Promised Land

*The 10 Commandments for Nonprofit
Strategy, Communications, and Fundraising*

Janet Cobb

Library of Congress Control Number: 2020924266
ISBN- 978-1-7362275-0-3

Dedication

To do-gooders around the globe—may you find your Promised Land.

Acknowledgements

Thanks to my husband Willie and my children Trey, Wilson and Janalie for the conversations and encouragement that helped to challenge and clarify my ideas.

Thanks to my many clients and workshop attendees who have shared their missions and visions, voiced concerns, asked questions and challenged me to articulate and clarify the ideas and tactics I've offered.

Thanks to the various do-gooders who shared their time and their expertise as early readers: Elizabeth Fallon Quilter, Rachel Ramjattan, Andrea Holthouser, and Andrea Finn.

Thanks to all who encouraged my efforts along the way: Kimberly O'Donnell, Kim Larison, T. Clay Buck, Tina Haller, Deidre Jordy, Ellen Kehl, Kathy Kessenich, Peg Quinn, and Cynthia Williams.

Introduction

Greetings, fellow do-gooder!

I've been called many names in my life, but the one I'm most proud of is "damn do-gooder." For some, the phrase implies idealism and naïveté, an overly simplistic view of building a better world. For the millions of people who have a passion for creating a better world AND work every day to bring that vision to reality (within and outside of the nonprofit arena), I say we must claim the name! We are do-gooders. We are not naïve; we are hopeful. We are not idealistic; we have high ideals. We know the complexity of the problems and the solutions that stand in the way of building a better world—yet, we persist.

If you've picked up this book, you're likely starting or working with a nonprofit organization as a board member, staff, or volunteer, with the hopes of bringing your vision for a better world to reality. Isn't that what starting or working with a nonprofit organization is all about—doing good in the world?

I know I'd rather be a do-gooder than a do-eviler, wouldn't you?

So, let's agree, you're a do-gooder. I'm a do-gooder. We're all do-gooders. And as do-gooders, we have serious business to tend to—problems to solve, communities to create, and souls to inspire.

Hopefully, this book offers insight into how you can put your heads and hearts together, think strategically to plan your work and work your plan and get to your Promised Land.

How I Got Here – Writing This Book

Recently, when a new client asked me how I got started in the nonprofit world, I was caught off guard. I had to think for a moment.

The nonprofit world has been part of my life for as long as I can remember, and since long before I knew what the word meant. From the moment my father abandoned my mother, leaving her to raise eight children alone, I survived on others' charity and goodness. Each holiday season, our family received the boxes of food from the food drives at the Catholic church, from which we also received financial assistance to attend school. I have vivid memories of receiving bags of clothes and furniture from classmates and the excitement of occasionally having a few dollars to purchase clothes at the local St. Vincent de Paul, a nonprofit resale shop. I lived in public housing, attended Head Start, received Free Lunch, participated in sponsored recreational programs and daycare centers, worked in youth employment programs for low-income teens, held car washes and bake sales to fund our programs, and attended Catholic school on scholarship.

My family was "the client story" organizations share to encourage donors to support their mission. I'd never heard the term "nonprofit." I simply knew that without the generosity of others, my life would have been far more difficult.

Missionaries showed up at school assemblies and Sunday Mass asking for support of their work with the poor, at home and abroad. Their presentations often moved me. One sticks out in my mind. After a Maryknoll missioner spoke, my mother urged me to give them money. "Since you have a job," she said. I casually and facetiously replied, "Nope. I might join 'em, but I'm not givin' em my money." The same missioner spoke in three different towns, where I happened to be visiting relatives over the next month.

In February 1982, six months after high school graduation, I entered a convent to become a Catholic sister, with a firm belief this would be the best way to spend my life doing good.

During my convent formation years, I lived and worked in a retreat house for women while I attended the local community college and helped local soup kitchens and homeless shelters from time to time. We served those in need of physical and spiritual sustenance and survived on the charitable donations of others.

On top of serving meals and maintaining the 55-room retreat center's housekeeping services, I was immediately immersed in the world of special events, donor appeals, and donor stewardship. I never thought of what we did as "nonprofit" work, but I wrote newsletters, direct mail appeals, and annual reports. I physically folded letters, stuffed and sealed envelopes, and licked stamps. I created marketing materials and brochures, sorted thousands of bulk mailing pieces by zip code across the long rectangular tables of our dining hall, and stood before church assemblies encouraging folks to register for retreats or support our work through calls-for-cash. We conducted a "Dollar-a-Month" club long before online giving was even imaginable, much less critical. Each month, we received hundreds of envelopes with one-dollar bills enclosed, often wrapped in a blank sheet of paper, for safety. Still, I didn't identify with the term "nonprofit."

Sent into the missions of Taiwan and Hong Kong in my early 20s, I witnessed and experienced poverty and simplicity, and wealth and prosperity in far more extreme disparity than I had ever seen as a child. In my youthful, radical adoption of the gospel, I rejected politics and believed in the simple power of love. Teaching high school during the Tiananmen Square Massacre, the Gulf War, the Vietnamese Refugee Crisis, and the pending Chinese control of Hong Kong, I got thrown into policy and advocacy issues. I found myself befriending the homeless on the streets, visiting the sick in hospitals, and protesting inequality. My desire to do good became more focused on challenging the injustices around me, both locally and globally. Issues like poverty alleviation, environmental awareness, racism, and nonviolence seeped into every classroom assignment and conversation, upending my equilibrium and driving me to challenge the status quo.

After thirteen years in religious life, for reasons far too complex to share here, I left the convent with a firm belief it was the best way for me to continue to spend my life doing good. Social justice issues continued to be a driving force in everything I did. I worked in nonprofit education, sat on boards and committees for strategic planning and capital campaigns, wrote grants for educational and technology programs, and designed appeals, newsletters, and annual reports with the hope of creating a better, more just, and equitable world.

I gradually moved from program delivery into fundraising and then into administration. In the executive director role, I became responsible for mission alignment and financial and program oversight. I navigated in board relations, donor relations, legal and risk management, and personnel issues. I'd worked my way from being a beneficiary of nonprofit services to running a nonprofit organization with an $8 million budget and 60 employees.

When personal and professional experiences forced me to rethink my life, and my career imploded just as my life in the convent had, I immersed myself in workshops, boot camps, webinars, and university courses. I received various certifications in starting and managing nonprofits, entrepreneurship, social impact enterprises, and business administration. I wasn't sure where my passion and do-gooder attitude would lead me, but I wanted to prepare.

Since 2014, I have coached more than 300 nonprofit founders, executive directors, and development professionals from across the United States on building their strategy, communications, and fundraising efforts—to realize their vision for a better world.

During my half-century immersed in the nonprofit arena, I've encountered challenges and opportunities and experienced success and failure. I've shared my knowledge and experience and gained tremendous insight along the way. I certainly don't know everything, but I hope that what I have come to understand will benefit others along the way to their Promised Land.

Why Title This Book *Promised Land*?

And I've looked over. And I've seen the promised land. I may not get there with you. But I want you to know tonight, that we, as a people will get to the Promised Land.
— Martin Luther King, Jr. April 3, 1968

Whether a nonprofit is secular, explicitly faith-based, or quietly faith-driven, the effort to do good is an attempt to bring the concepts of equality, freedom, peace, love, and care for neighbor and creation to life, practically and tangibly. Those working to do good in the world are fighting to bring about the *Beloved Community* popularized by Martin Luther King, Jr., all that the *Promised Land* meant for the descendants of Abraham, and the Q'uran's Jannah where there are gardens beneath which rivers flow.

The *Promised Land* represents a land flowing with milk and honey, where justice and mercy reigns, and peace resides. *Jannah* is the reward for living a just life, where everything is in its rightful place, and everyone receives their proper due. The *Beloved Community* represents an all-inclusive world that replaces racism and bigotry, and human decency will not allow poverty, hunger, and homelessness.

<u>*Promised Land*</u>: **A Three-Plan Approach**

If I had a nickel for every time a nonprofit founder or board member speculated on how all would be right with the world and their mission, if only they could bump into Oprah or Bill Gates in an elevator, I'd have as much money as Oprah or Bill Gates. Knowing this type of windfall is unlikely, they continue to dream of success, wish for big donors, and try to convince anyone who will listen to support their work rather than engage in the challenging work that is proven effective.

I've learned that when an organization engages in the **strategic planning** process (*Commandments 1-3*), develops a **communications plan** (*Commandments 5-7*), and integrates a **fundraising plan** (*Commandments 8-10*), they set the stage for organizational growth and a clear path for reaching their Promised Land.

Did you notice the three-plan approach outlined above doesn't include Commandment 4?

Don't worry. I didn't forget.

The 4th Commandment will focus on the importance of setting and respecting realistic boundaries to promote self-care and ward off burnout, which is a critical issue in the nonprofit sector. If we don't take care of ourselves and those around us, we cannot effectively implement the plans we develop or realize our vision.

Why Use the Ten Commandments Framework?

Given my familiarity with the Ten Commandments of the Jewish and Christian traditions, I believe this formula could be productive for several reasons:

- Many people are familiar with the construct and content of the Ten Commandments.
- The Ten Commandments correlate to many of the precepts and teachings of other major religions and philosophies and apply to most nonprofits' missions to do good in the world.
- The use of the "Thou Shall/Thou Shall Not" anaphora as a rhetorical device makes remembering the lessons easier.
- The shock value of framing nonprofit best practices and lessons within concepts like "Thou Shall Not Kill" and "Thou Shall Not Commit Adultery" will challenge the status quo a bit and offer a new perspective.

Who Should Read *Promised Land*?

If you're just beginning, or you've been wandering in the desert for years—this book's for you. If you're a do-gooder looking for inspiration and guidance—*Promised Land* is for you. If your nonprofit runs on a wing and a prayer, and your idea of a fundraising plan is to worship the golden calf—this book's for you. If you believe justice, mercy, and peace can reign, my wish for you is that these Ten Commandments lead you into your Promised Land.

The 1st Commandment
Thou SHALL have one mission.
Thou Shall NOT lose focus on your vision.

The 2nd Commandment
Thou SHALL NOT indulge in mission creep.
Thou SHALL make mission-centric decisions.

The 3rd Commandment
Thou shall NOT exist in vain.
Thou SHALL prepare for profitability.

The 4th Commandment
Thou SHALL keep holy the Sabbath.
Thou shall NOT burnout.

The 5th Commandment
Thou SHALL honor everyone.
Thou shall NOT brag about yourself.

The 6th Commandment
Thou shall NOT kill.
Thou SHALL foster a growth mindset.

The 7th Commandment
Thou shall NOT commit adultery.
Thou SHALL be loyal.

The 8th Commandment
Thou shall NOT steal.
Thou SHALL stop begging.

The 9th Commandment
Thou shall NOT bear false witness.
Thou SHALL be transparent.

The 10th Commandment
Thou shall NOT covet others' goods.
Thou SHALL keep calm and fundraise.

The Ten Commandments (Judaism & Christianity)	Yamas & Niyamas (Hinduism)	The Quran (Chapter: Verse)	The Ten Commandments for Nonprofits
Thou shall not take any God except one God.	*Ishvarapujana*: the return to the source	There is no God except one God (47:19)	Thou SHALL have ONE vision and mission. Thou Shall NOT indulge in mission creep.
Thou shall make no image of God.	*Ishvarapujana*: the cultivation of devotion through daily worship & meditation	There is nothing whatsoever like unto Him (42:11)	Thou shall NOT lose focus on your ONE vision. Thou SHALL manage your mission.
Thou shall not use God's name in vain.	*Shaucha*: purity, avoidance of impurity in body, mind, and speech	Make not God's name an excuse to your oaths (2:224)	Thou shall NOT exist in vain. Thou SHALL prepare for profitability.
Thou shall keep the Sabbath holy.	*Japa*: recitation, chanting mantras daily	When the call for the Friday Prayer is made, hasten to the remembrance of God and leave off your business. (62:9)	Thou SHALL keep holy the Sabbath. Thou shall NOT burnout.
Thou shall honor thy mother and father.	*Vrata*: sacred vows, fulfilling religious vows, rules, and observances faithfully *Daya*: compassion; conquering callous, cruel, and insensitive feelings toward all beings	Be kind to your parents if one or both of them attain old age in thy life, say not a word of contempt, nor repel them but address them in terms of honor. (17:23)	Thou SHALL honor everyone. Thou shall NOT brag about yourself.

Thou shall not kill.	*Ahisma*: nonviolence. abstinence from injury, harmlessness, the not causing of pain to any living creature in thought, word, or deed	If anyone has killed one person it is as if he had killed the whole mankind (5:32)	Thou shall NOT kill. Thou SHALL foster a growth mindset.
Thou shall not commit adultery.	*Asetya*: divine conduct, continence, celibate when single, faithful when married	Do not come near adultery. It is an indecent deed and a way for other evils. (17:32)	Thou shall NOT commit adultery. Thou SHALL be loyal.
Thou shall not steal.	*Asetya*: non-stealing, non-coveting, non-entering into debt	As for the thief, male or female, cut off his or her hands, but those who repent after a crime and reform shall be forgiven by God for God is forgiving and kind. (5:38-39)	Thou shall NOT steal. Thou SHALL stop begging.
Thou shall not lie or give false testimony.	*Satya*: truthfulness, word and thought in conformity with the facts	They invoke a curse of God if they lie. (24:7) Hide not the testimony (2:283)	Thou shall NOT bear false witness. Thou SHALL be transparent.
Thou shall not covet thy neighbors' wife or possessions.	*Arjava*: honesty, straightforwardness, renounce deception *Niyama*: Santosha - be satisfied with resources at hand - not desiring more	Do good to your parents, relatives, and neighbors. (4:36)	Thou shall NOT covet others' goods. Thou SHALL keep calm and fundraise.

Table of Contents

Part I: Strategy: Commandments 1 – 3

"A vision without a strategy remains an illusion."
Lee Bolman

*Quote: Bolman, L. G. and Deal, T. E. (2017). *Reframing Organizations: Artistry, Choice and Leadership, 6th ed., p. 205.* San Francisco: Jossey-Bass.

An old fundraising legend tells of a wealthy donor prepared to write a $1,000,000 check to an organization if they could meet one criterion. She attended a board meeting, requesting that the four executive officers sit in the four corners of the room to answer her question. She then quietly approached each and asked them, "What is your organization's current priority?"

After speaking with each officer, she promptly announced she could not donate to their organization because their answers were all different.

She visited one board meeting after another, with the same request. She spoke individually with executive officers about their top priority until she found one whose four officers responded the same. She happily donated $1,000,000 on the spot, believing her money would be put to good use because everyone in leadership understood and embraced the same priority. They would get things done with her money.

Although a legend, the reality is, if you never take the time to set your priorities and figure out how to share them with others, moving your mission forward will reflect a lack of direction at best, and, at worst, you will fail.

The Importance of a Plan

An acquaintance once said, "a business plan is the best work of fiction ever written." While this may be true, it is very tough to secure investments without a business plan. Investors want to know you've done your homework. If the entrepreneurial programs, pitch contests, and *Shark Tank* type competitions sweeping the country shed light on anything, it is this: you need a plan. People can get excited by an idea, but an idea without a plan is just a dream. The same holds for an organization's strategic plan. While Oprah or Bill Gates may love your idea, if you can't make your case and demonstrate you have a plan, you'll walk out with "the most famous person I've met" story but no money.

Doing your homework reduces the likelihood of mistakes that cost time and money. The final plan itself is not the critical piece, so much as the process of reviewing your current reality and developing methods to move you toward your vision. No matter how small or early-stage your organization, if done well, a strategic plan provides the qualitative and quantitative roadmap for where you are, where you're going, and how you'll get there.

If you think of your organization as a traditional rowing team, you know everyone needs to be rowing in the same direction at the same time. Otherwise, you aren't likely to get far. Who would bet on you? Your mission depends on folks betting on your organization to have a winning strategy.

You may think the board, executive director, and key staff members are all on the same page about your organizational priorities. A quick survey asking each person to share the organization's top priority might reveal striking results.

Try it! I dare you.

If everyone offers the same answer, kudos! If not, whether you employ a long, extensive method for identifying your priorities or you opt for a shortened, barebones approach, do something!

The 1st Commandment

Thou SHALL have one mission.
Thou Shall NOT lose focus on your vision.

You're probably thinking, "Yeah, yeah. One mission. No-brainer. Got it. We have a mission."

As do-gooders, we want to make the world a better place. So, we jump in to do good. Simple, right?

Wrong. If it were that simple, we'd all live in our Promised Land.

The United States has approximately 1.5 million recognized nonprofits. Each year, the IRS approves about 75,000 new 501(c)3 designated organizations. Yet, even with all these do-gooders, more can and still needs to be done.

The world still kinda sucks—for too many.

Worthy causes abound: the environment, education, health, justice, housing, animal welfare, and the arts. Since no one can do everything, do-gooders jump in to do something. Each do-gooder must decide what to do, who to help, why, when, where, and how to jump in. You decide what problem you'll solve, what improvement you'll bring, what service you'll offer. You might believe music, dance, painting, or theater make the world a better place to be. You could be interested in preserving history, promoting art appreciation, or protecting local or national treasures. You might feel passionately that the environment needs to be protected, children need education, homeless people need shelter, abused animals need rescuing, or we need to find a cure for cancer.

To identify your Promised Land, you'll need to move beyond a general awareness, concern, or passion to a clear vision for what COULD be and a plan for how you'll get there.

When I facilitate strategic planning processes with clients, I typically begin with a pre-session survey to help jumpstart the conversation. The survey asks board members to write their organization's mission from memory (without peeking at documents, minutes, or the website).

One response a few years back is especially memorable. The small organization was celebrating its 10th anniversary, yet one long-standing board member responded to this question with, "I have no idea." While this is an extreme example, no matter the organization's size, age, programs, or how long a member has been on the board, the answers are typically as varied as the number of people responding. I've never had identical responses from everyone.

Don't get me wrong. Even the youngest and most dysfunctional nonprofits have some type of written mission statement—good or not so good. The statements are often weakly stated, hesitant, complicated, and not easily remembered. Too many fumble their words, muddle through "we know we'll never get there, but we'll keep trying" attitudes, and search for how to explain what they do. They struggle to sum up their mission and the difference they hope to make in a few words.

Articulating your mission in a clear, concise, easy-to-remember manner is challenging—but critical. We can't fulfill our mission if we aren't certain what it is. How will we find others to commit to the mission? More importantly, how will we know when we've accomplished it?

This confusion around mission often lies in the fact that we haven't clearly articulated our vision.

Vision: What is Your Promised Land?

Your vision is what the world (or your corner of it) will look like when you can say "mission accomplished." What is the result of the work you do? What would the world look like if you had your way?

Martin Luther King Jr. envisioned a Beloved Community of justice and equality. Malala Yousufzai, a Muslim, advocates for, at the very least, the education of girls. Gandhi, a Hindu, "fasted unto death" to protest India's caste system. Mother Teresa of Calcutta wanted everyone, even the least loveable in society, to experience love. The Tank Man stared down tanks rolling into Tiananmen Square to fight for democracy. For Moses, the Promised Land meant freedom from oppression for the Israelites, in a land flowing with milk and honey.

Most small nonprofits will not likely reach the notoriety of Martin, Mahatma Gandhi, Moses, Malala, Mother Teresa, or the Tank Man. Like many activists across the globe, from a wide variety of non-religious and religious backgrounds, your vision of the Promised Land can be achieved in small doses, small spaces, and without publicity and still change the world.

Articulate Your WHY

I often begin my client relationships by asking a simple question, "Why?" Why do you exist? And I keep asking, like a toddler, until the nonprofit leader I'm speaking with gets to the core of why their organization exists. I asked this of a new client last week, who responded, "Because there are homeless people in our county and there shouldn't be." Her vision was clear, and her vision that no one in her county should remain homeless drives every decision the young organization makes.

Many folks might share a similar vision when it comes to a cause—who doesn't want world peace? Or a cure for cancer? Or the end to homelessness and hunger? Not everyone working for a cause or focus area will necessarily share the same vision in their work.

Consider, for example, different aspects around the cause of homelessness. We may all envision a world where no one is homeless. At the same time, we might recognize homelessness results from a combination of political, economic, social, and mental health issues that could take years or decades to solve.

One do-gooder will address these complexities through advocacy to get affordable housing policy implemented or improvements to mental health care or increases to the minimum wage to prevent homelessness. Another do-gooder might focus on ensuring those who are homeless right now and, in the future, have shelter, available sanitation, coats, shoes, food, and job skills training, as needed. One's vision is housing for all; the other's is care for all homeless people. Until no one is homeless, both are needed. Until then, one doesn't negate the other.

Think of organizations whose cause is related to a specific disease: diabetes, any one of many cancers, or mental illness. You're probably thinking, "Of course, we want to eradicate the disease!" Until then, many organizations might have other visions. A vision might be that treatment is found, everyone understands the risk factors leading to the disease, or those diagnosed with the disease receive the emotional support they need.

Take, for example, three nationwide cancer-related organizations. *Susan G. Komen*'s vision is "a world without breast cancer" (komen.org). *Gilda's Club*'s vision is that no one faces cancer alone. *Cleaning for a Reason* cleans— *until there is a cure*. One allocates resources to finding a cure. One ensures those impacted by cancer are "empowered by knowledge, strengthened by action, and sustained by community" (gildasclubkc.org). One engages cleaning services across the country and Canada to clean the homes of those undergoing cancer treatment.

Maybe your vision is to bring beautiful and inspiring art, literature, or theater to your community, and you don't think of it as a problem at all. You'll still find clarity by asking why you exist and what you want to do for your community. *Karin Stevens Dance* investigates the complex layers of our cultural spaces, time, and relationship to earth (karinstevensdance.com). *Neglia Ballet* is committed to preserving the artistry, technique, and traditions of ballet through high-quality performance and superior instruction (negliaballet.org). Fort Wayne, Indiana's *all for One Production Company* impacts our culture for God through the arts (allforonefw.org). *The Hub Arts and Cultural Center* works to create and maintain a connection between the arts, rural culture, and our local communities through exhibitions and educational experiences (thehubart.com). Each organization works to enrich their community through the arts in some way (their *cause*); they each understand it differently (their *vision*) and implement it in a unique (their *mission*).

Regardless of your cause, the desired outcome dictates the organization's approach, programs, and priorities. The vision determines the mission.

Mission happens when we articulate the problem we hope to address, the solution we hope to offer, and the impact we hope to have. Understanding our WHY and stating the problem and solution defines the reason for and nature of our existence.

Identify Your Mission

Mission happens when you explore, articulate, and implement steps to achieve your vision so you can effectively address the cause or problem you face. Are you trying to get at the root cause of a problem—like curing cancer? Will you foster self-confidence and resilience in children through arts education and entertainment? Will you change systems that cause a problem—like homelessness? Will you research, advocate, prevent, educate, or serve those impacted? In other words:

- What do you do?
- How do you do it?
- What impact do (or will) you have?

Sample Vision and Mission Statements

The Seraj Library Project's vision is "access to a community library for every Palestinian child and family" (11 words). Their mission, "In partnership with Seraj Palestine, Seraj US exists to establish and enrich community libraries for Palestinian children and their families" (20 words). (serajlibraries.org)

CLEAN International's vision is "an end to the daily walk for water worldwide and the eradication of waterborne illness" (15 words). Therefore, the organization "mobilizes and evaluates innovative, environmentally sustainable solutions for clean water and sanitation through ongoing education, partnerships, and evaluation in order to save and improve lives" (24 words). (cleaninternational.org)

Move United (a recent merge of Adaptive Sports USA and Disability Sports USA) has a vision that "every person, regardless of ability, has an equal opportunity to participate in sports and recreation in their community" (18 words). Their mission is "to provide national leadership and opportunities for individuals with disabilities to develop independence, confidence, and fitness through participation in community sports, competition, recreation, high performance sport and educational programs" (29 words). (moveunitedsport.org)

Wondermore "envision a world in which all children have the opportunity to see themselves in the books they read and are inspired to become lifelong learners" (25 words). Their mission "connects Boston-area students to authors and illustrators of children's books who reflect our diverse communities" (15 words). (wondermoreboston.org)

Habitat for Humanity's vision is "a world where everyone has a decent place to live" (10 words). Their mission, "seeking to put God's love into action, Habitat for Humanity brings people together to build homes, communities and hope" (19 words). (habitat.org)

A Mission Must Be Unique

Many do-gooders care about the same cause, but no two organizations share the exact same mission. Articulating your mission involves analyzing the issue, identifying the need, deciding your point of entry, and offering your best solution. What makes you distinct and different from another organization's mission? Each mission must have a unique fingerprint. What makes your mission unique? Why is your mission necessary right here, right now?

A Mission Must Matter

Your mission must matter.

Each mission must add value.

If your organization closed your doors tomorrow, never to reopen, would anyone be worse off (besides employees who'll lose their jobs) because you don't exist? How many lives would be severely, negatively impacted? How much more terrible would the world be?

If you can resoundingly shout in the face of the one suggesting you disband, "That would be horrible because _____ (fill in the blank with a compelling reason)," then your mission matters!

If, on the other hand, you struggle to articulate decisively WHO (animals and environment included) will suffer if your organization didn't exist and WHY or HOW they would suffer, you could benefit from conducting a comprehensive mission and vision articulation exercise.

If your non-existence would simply be an inconvenience or a blip on the screen because others could fill in the gap, you would do well to consider merging with

11

the organization that would fill the gap if you leave. Or to be frank, consider disbanding. On that note, if your existence is absolutely necessary, but you could better accomplish your vision if you merged with one or other organizations, please consider merging.

After all, do-gooder, the point isn't to simply exist but to get to the point where you can announce, "mission accomplished." If that can happen sooner, rather than later, make it happen!

When you know and can explain the damage caused if your organization went away, you're further articulating your WHY. WHY is the issue you focus on critical? WHY do you address this problem, this aspect of the issue? WHY do you do what you do, when you do it, where you do it, how you do it? WHY do you offer your solution? WHY do you _not_ do something else or offer it somewhere else? WHY does your mission matter?

If your non-existence would simply be an inconvenience or a blip on the screen, you would do well to consider merging with the organization that would fill the gap if you leave—or, to be frank, consider disbanding.

Articulate Your Scope

In defining your mission, considering your scope helps define your programs and services, your reach and impact, and sometimes, who else will care to join your cause.

Service Scope

Every nonprofit mission addresses one or more of Abraham Maslow's hierarchal pyramid of needs so many of us learned in high school psychology. In the 1940s, Abraham Maslow outlined five levels of need ranging from the most basic physiological needs to full self-actualization. Some experts debate the merits of his theory or whether the levels intersect or have permeable boundaries. Nevertheless, the pyramid reminds us, do-gooders, that each level matters—and so does each scope of service. Understanding the differences helps us to stay focused on our services and messaging.

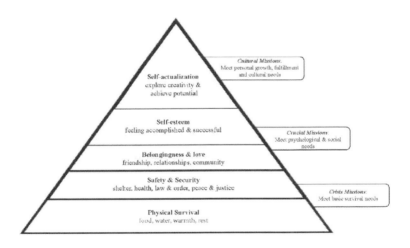

• *Crisis Missions*

Crisis missions have an inherent urgency addressing what Maslow calls every individual's physiological and safety needs: food, water, warmth, rest, security. These missions provide services like aid in a natural disaster, food for children, care for the homeless, protection for victims of abuse, emergency medical attention for those who need it. If these actions aren't taken, someone will die.

- *Crucial Missions*

Crucial missions, while urgent, do not address life or death, but rather the psychological need to belong, fit in, build relationships, and feel a sense of accomplishment. These missions' services and activities move us from physical survival to emotional well-being and address quality of life rather than protecting life itself. These missions might include education, workforce development, physical fitness and athletic programs, affinity groups, or religious organizations.

- *Cultural Missions*

Cultural missions focus on self-actualization and self-fulfillment, addressing life enrichment and personal development concerns. These missions include visual and performing arts, museums, theaters, and historical societies. These organizations provide services that move a community from mere existence to creativity, enrichment, and innovation where individuals thrive.

In a perfect, all-encompassing Promised Land, every basic need would be met, and everyone would achieve their full potential. As do-gooders, we know whether a mission addresses critical needs, crucial concerns, or cultural enrichment, ONE mission is not less worthy than another. But as you articulate your ONE mission, being aware of these distinctions will help you express your WHY and gravitate toward others who believe in and care about what you care about.

Clients will sometimes bemoan that fundraising is difficult because they don't have compelling pictures of sad children or puppies—their mission isn't sexy. Imagine a world where only the most basic human physical needs are met, leaving us without the beauty of emotional and spiritual connectedness or any sense of creativity or fulfillment.

No one wants to merely exist. The world needs missions offering non-critical products and services to remind us—life means more than only surviving.

Geographic Scope

Without getting into a debate about quantum physics, string theory, and the possibility of parallel universes, fundamental physics dictates that a mission exists at one point in time and space. Even with the wonders of technology and globalization that allows for the instantaneous sharing of information and connectedness (with an unlimited number of people) across mountains, deserts, and seas, I think of organizations as falling into one of several geographic scopes: community-based, local, global, or universal.

While an organization's location does not determine its mission's geographic scope, the geographic scope allows you to consider various governance structures, mission parameters, and fundraising intentions. Your geographic scope will also influence how far and how quickly your mission will spread and, in some cases, who else might care.

- *Place-based*

A place-based or community-based organization recognizes opportunities for growth and improvement within a community, commonly around economic development and the need for improved services within a relatively small geographic location. I won't attempt to replace or minimize the books experts have written and the institutes developing and teaching Asset-Based Community Development. If your vision is to improve or strengthen a community, if you have not already, I encourage you to explore this model as you articulate or revise your vision and mission (www.nurturedevelopment.org/asset-based-community-development). For our purposes here, I offer questions for the strategic planning process to address possible opportunities for growth with regards to incorporating principles of this placed-based, asset-based development model.

Do your vision and mission demonstrate belief in the strengths, insights, and possibility of community members to design and determine their communities' progress? Do your governance and organizational structures exhibit your confidence in the capacity for growth within your community members? Do you value the perspectives community members bring to the discussion of the issues? Are the leadership team members proximate to the work you do, or are they outsiders looking into a community to fix it? Is your leadership representative of the community you serve? Do your policies and programs encourage collaboration between institutions and agencies in the community? Do programs lead to personal empowerment? Do your fundraising strategies and communications endorse a deficit or asset-based approach to growth?

- *Local*

Your vision might be local but not focused on community development. You may be offering enrichment lessons, arts or sports programs, adult literacy classes, or hospice care. You might run a museum, neighborhood association, or community theater. Any number of products or services not directly connected to community development can have a local focus. These organizations will sometimes expand to a national footprint, usually through organizational replication (or independent chapter model), but their efforts remain locally focused for the most part.

Like an artist's home-turned-museum or a point of historical interest, some organizations are local, but its WHY often reaches well beyond the region. The *Grace Hudson Museum & Sun House*, for example, is located in Ukiah, California, at the home of the artist, Grace Hudson, and her husband. People from all over the country (and the world) visit to learn about the artist and appreciate her work. The *Eastland Disaster Historical Society* preserves the history and stories of the 844 individuals (including 22 entire families) who died in a boat accident on the Chicago River on July 24, 1915. In their efforts, they've connected with families worldwide whose relatives and loved ones perished on that tragic day. Neither of these two locations will move, which means they are geographically local, but their impact extends far beyond their region.

- *International*

Your vision might be international if you're working to address the global refugee crisis, provide clean drinking water, or facilitate medical services in emergencies. For example, the *Novick Cardiac Alliance* is committed to improving the skills, knowledge, technology, and experience of local health-care providers without access to quality Pediatric Cardiac Care (cardiac-alliance.org). These missions reach across communities and countries to meet a need, and their geographic location does not confine them.

- *Universal*

Universal missions are less about working in a particular place and more about creating a movement. Folks from across the globe can get behind the vision and mission to halt global warming, support LGBTQIA+ rights, cure cancer, or fight domestic violence, no matter where they are.

Just as your service scope impacts your vision and mission, your geographic scope will determine how your mission will grow (strategy), how you will demonstrate impact (communications), and who will be interested in supporting you (fundraising).

Market Research

If you are in the early founding stages of your nonprofit or you're in the process of reevaluating your programs and services for the strategic planning process, conducting thorough market research will be very beneficial.

Strategic planners often conduct a SWOT analysis by asking, "What are our strengths, weakness, opportunities, and threats?" Opportunities and threats are factors outside of your organization. Strengths and weaknesses are internal factors. When you ask how they impact your ability to deliver and fulfill your mission effectively, you begin to ask the right market research questions.

Remember the "who would fill the gap if we don't exist" reflection we just went through? That is a market research question. To define the problem's scope or the opportunity for growth, you'll want to ask, "Who and how many people need or want our product/service?" Keep going with questions like: Is anyone already working on this problem? What solution are they providing? What is its impact? Will we offer an innovative solution? An upgrade or shift to an existing approach? How many people do they serve? Will we serve the same group or a different group? Who is our customer base?

You'll also want to consider if you'll be building relationships with the same potential donors. What might distinguish your prospective donor pool from an existing organizations' donor base? Do you have the capacity to provide products and services in a meaningful way, given your prospective customer and donor base? How many people will need to be involved in delivery? What skill sets will they need? How will they be trained and retained?

Carefully thinking through these types of market research questions will leave you with more precise goals and objectives and a much greater chance to achieve them during a strategic planning process. Remember, this approach is useful for launching an entirely new organization or simply introducing or adapting a new program element.

I'll never forget Margaret, the newly hired American principal at the school where I taught in Hong Kong, which served 1200 local Chinese students. She was horrified they still had drop toilets requiring students to squat over the porcelain bowl mounted in the floor. One of her first decisions as the new principal was to replace all the toilets in the building with western-style tank and commode models. She then spent the next six months complaining about the little shoe prints on the toilet seats. She didn't realize students would heed their parents' warnings to never sit on a public toilet, even at school. She had solved a problem that didn't exist because she had neglected to ask students and parents if squat toilets were a problem needing to be solved.

I've encountered more than one do-gooder who, like Margaret, thinks they know what needs to be done, but they fail to conduct the necessary research or to listen to the constituents they are hoping to serve.

I briefly worked with an organization that consistently conducted exit interviews to garner feedback from program participants. I was excited—until the ED explained that more than 90% of participants would prefer not to rotate between three or four sites for services every week. She wouldn't change the rotation because it kept the volunteers engaged and feeling important. My heart sank. They'd undergone the research but refused to hear the voices of those they serve.

When you neglect to conduct market research or ignore the results, your vision and mission suffer. You may sink a good deal of time and energy, not to mention financial resources, into your way of doing things—your solution—all to no avail.

Minimum Viable Product

When COVID-19 hit in Winter/Spring 2020, the world scrambled to implement new "hows" to meet their "whys" and "whats." The vision and mission didn't change for most nonprofits, but the delivery of their solution certainly did.

While everyone needed to adjust, for many nonprofit arts organizations, theaters, and museums that rely heavily on in-person interactions, discovering new ways to fulfill the mission was a challenge needing innovative solutions. Organizations serving populations hard-hit by the pandemic were suddenly called upon to provide food and financial assistance to those they previously offered job training, education, or enrichment opportunities. Many were at a loss for how to move forward. My recommendation was to brainstorm new ideas, pick one or two to try, start small, and go from there. I had to convince some of my small and early-stage organizations not to allow their solution to become an obstacle. Instead, they needed to return to their mission and ask how else they could accomplish it.

The *Food Equality Initiative* in Kansas City first turned their allergen-free food pantry service into a pick-up process and then a delivery service. With rapid success in door-to-door delivery for recipients in their area, they soon realized that forming a partnership with a distribution company would allow them to scale and reach an entirely new market. Soon they had folks across the country asking how to start a chapter in their state or county. Their small shop is quickly going national because they kept asking a fundamental question, "How can we BEST serve the community to fulfill our mission?"

In the start-up world, the concept of a minimum viable product (MVP) and proof of concept are critical steps to building a business model and securing funding to bring a product or service to the market. An MVP answers the question, "what is the least we can do" to serve our customers and learn from their engagement and experience with our product or service. With trial and error and improvements along the way, you work to make it better and then the best.

As a do-gooder, you determine your MVP by deciding how you will begin to test your solution. To address hunger, you could distribute sandwiches at the local homeless community encampment, offer a free meal from a church hall, gather donations for a food basket during the holiday season, or help someone unemployed find a job so they can buy their own food. If you want music education to be available to every child in the school district, your MVP might be lessons for a small group of students at one school for a limited time. If you want to help people find jobs, you could work with a handful of unemployed people to test what works and what doesn't. If you're going to build wells in remote villages in South America, identify one village and work with them to determine what they need and how to make it happen.

You begin with your MVP so as you offer programs and services, you can also gather data, reflect on your solution, and tweak and pivot, as needed, to find the best solution for fulfilling your mission.

Mission vs. Solution

Remember, do-gooder, an important point to consider when identifying or revisiting your vision and mission is that your solution does not equal your mission. What you do and how you do it can be adjusted to get closer to your vision. You always want to be looking into how you can get to the next level of excellence. Too often, we get so caught up in the solution, we forget the WHY. But the vision is the WHY you and others show up each day. The vision and mission are WHY donors support you.

If you've identified a better route to get where you're ultimately trying to go, don't let your current solution keep you stuck on the wrong track. On the flip side, be careful not to fall victim to mission creep.

The 2nd Commandment

Thou SHALL NOT indulge in mission creep.
Thou SHALL make mission-centric decisions.

If you're like many do-gooders, especially those providing critical services, you can sometimes feel like your solution only chips away at the tip of a vast, hidden iceberg of a problem.

Frustrated or eager or ambitious, you start reaching a little further and a bit deeper, hoping to have a more significant impact. A pig rescue decides to take in dogs; a homeless shelter directs resources to fight the root causes of homelessness. An organization providing care packages to those fighting breast cancer decides to support stomach or lung cancer patients. While these new endeavors aren't bad things, you need to double-check your priorities so you aren't allowing mission creep to undermine your ONE mission's effectiveness.

Over-extending can be tempting, particularly if you're solving problems at the lower levels of Maslow's pyramid because the factors creating physical and psychological need can be very complex and interwoven. Remember, offering an excellent, impactful, and effective solution to one problem can often be better than providing half-baked, sloppy, and ineffective solutions to many problems.

Build a strong foundation. Begin with your MVP, prove your concept, and keep the mission at the center of every decision. Don't stray. But don't stagnate either.

Lifecycles

Like all living organisms, every organization goes through cycles. Any internet search will result in plenty of analogies comparing an organization to an individual's lifecycle: birth, growth from childhood to adolescence, maturity in adulthood. Few, if any, will focus on the taboo subject of an organization's decline, i.e., the years before death.

When an organization tries to do too much too quickly without focusing on ONE mission, it could struggle to thrive. The same holds if it doesn't do enough or adapt to changing opportunities or societal or environmental threats.

Some organizations realize a steady increase in program size and success, accompanied by an expansion of size and infrastructure (exponential growth) early on or shortly after the start-up phase. At some point, this growth plateaus and efforts focus on maintaining program operations (logistic growth) in fits and starts.

For many organizations, particularly those with compelling and cultural missions (as opposed to crisis missions), this logistic growth can only be sustained for so long before it hits the crossroad of choice: do something to keep people coming back—or die. How will you offer a fresh perspective? How will you encourage and embody rebirth? How will the mission attract new supporters?

Often the answer is simple: improve practice and process. In other words, change what you're doing.

Change

Changing for change's sake is not only pointless but can be detrimental. At the same time, resisting change because it's "never been done before" is costly. Change is inevitable.

New technologies, webinars, and workshops, and best of the best lists bombard you, convincing you that incorporating this or that tactic will send you on your way to new donors and success in meeting your goals.

Don't fall prey to the quick fix or the fear of missing out (FOMO, which we'll discuss further in the 10th Commandment) on the latest idea. Instead of chasing every trendy opportunity, be deliberate in adopting new methods, particularly when it comes to fundraising and donor engagement. Why are you making this change? What do you hope to accomplish? How will you measure success? How does it help your mission?

Approaching change with somewhat reckless abandon by randomly throwing solutions at a problem to see what might stick can be more wasteful and deadly than no change at all. Your present reality should not limit your future possibility but chasing possibility without a plan to evaluate success and impact is futile.

Avoid Mission Creep

You always want to continue to improve and grow. Staying focused on ONE mission doesn't mean you stagnate. If you simply start adding program elements without having a clear plan for sustainable growth, you could find yourself doing more but not necessarily have a more significant impact.

A strategic planning process can lead to insights and discovery of how best to approach the next level of excellence. When you realize your solution needs to be different or better, you find yourself at a crossroads due to new circumstances, or you've accomplished one set of goals and need another.

Although you have many options for how to grow, I think most organizations find themselves falling into one of five categories: maintain the current status, go deep, pivot, replicate, or join forces.

Maintain

Ultimately, remaining true to your ONE mission to feed the hungry or support a person living with a specific disease or offering afterschool science programs—or whatever your mission might be—is perfectly valid. You *maintain* your service, knowing you cannot solve every problem, but you can meet one need in this space and time, for the time being, and fulfill ONE mission. On your watch, no one in your town will go hungry. On your watch, someone living with this disease in your city will not fend for themselves alone. On your watch, children in your community will have access to quality afterschool science programs.

Your strategic goals, then, do-gooder, will be to focus on consistently improving your solution. You'll want to ensure that all those who would benefit from your product or service have access. You'll need to fight against complacent thought patterns like "good enough." Never be satisfied with the status quo. Would your board, staff, or volunteers benefit from new training? Are there new or innovative ways to deliver your solution? Do you engage in conversation with your beneficiaries to ask their opinions about your mission delivery?

Go Deep

When you find yourself at an impact plateau, you may be driven to *go deep*. Regardless of where you begin on Maslow's pyramid, you'll be looking across arenas to *go deep*. If you work in a crisis mission, this might mean you aren't satisfied until you meet each person's critical physiological and safety needs and eradicate the root causes. You might not be satisfied with merely meeting these basic needs. If your mission operates in the area of crucial services, you'll push for cultural mission services for your community.

If you offer cultural products and services, have you thought about how you can benefit individuals who are still struggling to satisfy their critical and crucial needs? To *go deep* means to explore how to offer the full spectrum of services so your community not only survives but thrives.

Yeah, I hear you shouting, "But you said to avoid mission creep! Now you're telling us to creep across mission scope!"

The critical point here is that you make a strategic decision to *go deep* only AFTER you've reached capacity with the solutions you currently offer. During a strategic planning process, you're looking for opportunities for continued impact and transformational change.

Inspiration Kitchen in Chicago began with one woman distributing sandwiches from a little red wagon and developed into a job-training program for previously incarcerated individuals who currently operate full-functioning, high-quality restaurants and catering services. This organization went deeper than feeding the homeless by creating a solution to address the causes so fewer people would be homeless. They were intentional and strategic.

The *Garces Foundation* provides English language courses and medical/dental support to the immigrant population in Philadelphia. When participants lost their jobs because of COVID-19, the Foundation quickly began providing food boxes, so those who previously served others in restaurants would have food to put on their own tables. They went deeper to meet fundamental needs in a time of crisis. They understood that participants wouldn't have the mental and emotional wherewithal without food on their tables to continue their education and personal growth.

Pivot

The word *pivot* is essential to the discussion of strategic growth because, as a noun, *pivot* represents the center or focal point, the hinge, the fulcrum, and as a verb, it means to revolve around a center point. Unlike mission creep or a detour that could lead a do-gooder or an organization entirely off the rails related to their mission and vision, when you *pivot*, you remain linked to the original WHY.

In 1985, *Bryan's House* in Dallas, Texas, began its mission to offer medically managed childcare for children living with HIV/AIDS. With medical advances in the treatment of HIV/AIDS, over time, the need for these services decreased. Bryan's House had already proven their medically-supported childcare model provided a much-needed service for families facing other medical crises. They could have opted to phase out their services, announced "mission accomplished," and ceased operations.

Instead, they decided to *pivot* to provide their proven care model to children and families struggling with a wide variety of medical issues. Bryan's House revised their mission statement to welcome infants and toddlers with chronic and acute conditions beyond AIDS, to address the growing need, and to use the resources they had readily available.

Replicate

Much like the franchise model in business, some organizations create a service model in one location that someone can then replicate in another. They might simply open a second location. Or they could establish a chapter, membership, or affiliation model with independent boards and executive directors adhering to a national vision and mission.

In entrepreneurial language, what we're talking about is scale. When you are just beginning, you may not be thinking about replicating your model. And being intentional to demonstrate proof of concept and impact before you spread yourself too thin is a good thing. I like to caution my clients to not be in a hurry (more about this in the 4th commandment). That said, if you're providing a valuable product or service and having a positive impact, why not make it available to more folks, right?

Examples of organizations that have replicated abound. To name just a few:

- *Ronald McDonald House Charities* provides lodging for the families of those in long-term medical treatment at and near hospitals across the country.
- *Family Promise* is an association of communities supporting families facing homelessness with

temporary room and board while they get back on their feet.

- *Court Appointed Special Advocates* (CASA) trains volunteers to accompany and advocate for children in the foster care system in nearly 1000 state and county offices.
- *Boys and Girls Clubs* offer safe spaces for kids to learn and play in all 50 states, U.S. territories, and on U.S. military bases around the world.

Two I've personally watched grow from their early stages are *Common Threads* (commonthreads.org), which fights childhood obesity by teaching cooking classes to children in several states, and *The Simple Good* (thesimplegood.org), which works to connect the meaning of "good" across the globe through art and discussion.

These services each began in one space and time. So, do-gooder, if you'd love to see an expansion of your impact and you know your solution works, why not do more good in more places? By all means, go for it!

Join Forces

We'll talk later (See 10th Commandment) about the dangers of being competitive in the nonprofit arena. For now, I think it's important to remind all of us do-gooders that accomplishing the vision and reaching the Promised Land is more important than one organization or another surviving. If we can create a transformational impact by *joining forces*, our moral and ethical obligation is to do so.

For example, four organizations in California's Tahoe/Truckee region had each been doing great work to serve the local community's critical needs for many years.

Tahoe SAFE Alliance addressed domestic violence and sexual assault. *Project MANA* fed the hungry. *North Tahoe Family Resource Center* and the *Family Resource Center of Truckee* offered social and legal services and support to their respective communities. In 2017, they realized they could increase their impact in the local community by merging. The process has been complicated and has taken time, but on July 1, 2019, the four officially became *Sierra Community House.*

By *joining forces*, they better serve the community because many of those needing one of their services also need another. They are further improving their beneficiaries' lives, not to mention their staff and volunteers, by becoming more effective and efficient. Each organization offered one aspect of the critical physiological and safety/security needs of Maslow's pyramid. By *joining forces*, fewer individuals and families will fall through the cracks, and they'll create a more stable community. As a larger organization, they've been better able to respond to the COVID-19 pandemic wreaking havoc on their small tourism-dependent town. They have become the sole crisis response agency in the area.

Whether *joining forces* means officially merging to become a new entity like *Sierra Community House* or merely working together to coordinate services, when you explore the opportunities for growth during your strategic planning process, please don't reject the option to *join forces.*

Let Your Mission Be Your Mantra

Unlike the financial bottom line driving many for-profit business decisions, every decision you make in a nonprofit organization needs to stay laser-focused on your ONE vision and mission. Although one of the board's primary responsibilities is to ensure the organization's long-term viability, and finances can't be ignored, the financial returns should not be the focal point of any decision. Every decision should serve to further the vision and mission.

Even if, at some point, you go deeper, pivot, replicate or join forces and your mission shifts, the shift becomes your new ONE mission and must come first. At this point, don't let anything get in your way or divert your attention. Your vision and mission must permeate the culture of your organization.

In many ways, this sounds like a no-brainer. I've seen too many do-gooders make decisions that are more aligned with the will and whims of a board member, executive director, or program officer than with the vision and mission. I'm not implying any malice here. Most individuals who work in and with nonprofit organizations have a good heart and pure intentions. Most are trying to do good. Sometimes, the very desire to do good, or personalities and biases, cloud our judgment and making vision and mission-centric decisions challenging.

Tough Decisions

Reaching unanimous support for policies, procedures, and programs is rarely simple.

A wise mentor once cautioned that when two people cannot agree on how to solve a problem, three possible solutions likely exist: my way, their way, and the best way.

Always focusing on how each decision impacts the mission is an effective method to interrupt and uplift conversations that might otherwise devolve into the weeds of minutiae or allow personality conflict, power struggles, and personal agendas to derail progress.

Discussion

A discussion is simply an exchange of opinions and points of fact—sometimes to reach a decision. Ideally, everyone has an opportunity to voice their opinions in a discussion, and each listens to the other. After a discussion, the deciding action is usually a *majority wins* voting process. Those who don't win, lose. This process may or may not result in the best mission-centric decision.

Discernment

Discernment is a process by which members of a group listen to one another's concerns in a respectful manner, attempting to understand and empathize with one another in the hopes of reaching a consensus. Discernment is rooted in the belief that the group will find wisdom through communication and reach unanimity and harmony of opinion. You may need to compromise, but through this process, no one wins or loses because no decision is made until everyone agrees on the best next steps.

Decisions

Many bylaws outline the voting process for the board, with details of when participants must be notified of a vote and determining what constitutes a majority. These details often create a contentious, win-lose mentality encouraging legalistic, transactional approaches to decisions. Even within the traditional bylaw format, the board can decide to work towards consensus, adopting a discernment process before voting.

You can undoubtedly make decisions without discernment, and voting may be the easiest and quickest way to reach a decision. When you make decisions without discernment, and consensus is not the end goal, a win-lose mentality can persist. Individuals can hold on to personal agendas, which leaves some participants feeling ignored or dismissed. Someone may still walk away, not agreeing with the decision.

Committing to discernment and reaching consensus, particularly when amending the mission and vision during a strategic planning process, encourages engagement. Discernment and consensus might take much longer than voting, but everyone would be able to articulate how and why any decision is the best decision to further the ONE vision and mission.

• *Person Independent Decisions*

We must remember the vision and the mission aren't about any one individual. I've seen too many organizations struggling to move forward because the executive director or board chair controls all the decisions with others simply rubber-stamping everything. Other times the policies, organization charts, job descriptions, and programs are based on the skills, talents, strengths, and limitations of current staff instead of being for the mission's overall good.

I've worked with too many clients who stagnate because people don't know how, or are afraid, to hold other board members or staff accountable. They are afraid to institute self-assessment or evaluation criteria because they don't want to offend anyone's feelings. Board members hesitate to hold an executive director or founder accountable because they have been in the organization for years. Fears of offending someone's feelings, rocking the boat, or upsetting folks can cause an organization to muddle along for years, making little progress because somewhere along the way made a wrong decision, and now no one wants to undo it.

In all too many organizations, the founder hangs around too long, holding the vision and mission tightly to their chests, giving the organization no room to breathe. Rather than allowing the mission to thrive, they embody what's come to be known as "founder's syndrome." Founder's syndrome is not always the fault of a zealous, passionate visionary who set about changing the world. Their love for the work they put into motion is understandable and admirable.

Problems arise when board members and others allow the founder to do so much of the heavy lifting regarding donor cultivation and stewardship, relationship building, strategic and visionary thinking that if the founder walked away tomorrow, they'd be like a boat without a rudder. And suppose the founder has been in a position to offer their services for little to no salary. In this case, this can leave the organization in a real financial pickle if the budget can't handle a salaried position to replace the founder's volunteer services.

- *Financial Decisions*

Financial decisions need to focus on the bottom line to ensure the organization's fiscal viability, but they must also flow from a mission-centric perspective. When money gets tight because programs don't thrive, mistakes are made, and decisions get muddled. Keeping your mission and vision front and center is critical to making sound business decisions. Mission-centric decisions are more likely to inspire support and move the organization closer to the vision than a cut-to-succeed or deficit fundraising approach.

Sometimes cuts will need to be made. Mission-centric discussions will still get heated and passionate. Staying focused on how best to fulfill the mission tends to raise the rhetoric to philosophical beliefs, values, and decision-making rather than personal agendas, egos, and personalities.

When the Coronavirus (COVID-19) struck a blow to life as we know it, many nonprofit organizations scrambled to rethink, reconfigure, and readjust service delivery within the confines of shelter-in-place, work-from-home, physical distancing, and wearing masks. Those organizations that continually asked themselves how they could further the mission seem to be weathering the storm. They could identify their priorities, communicate them clearly to their communities, and keep moving forward amid a confusing and anxious time.

Keep your vision and mission front and center

When facing challenging questions, we must keep the mission and vision front and center. The strategic planning process allows you to consistently ask, "how does this further the mission and get us closer to the Promised Land" and help you avoid some of the landmines populating many nonprofit board rooms. When those sitting in the boardroom disagree on key policy and budget issues and internal personality conflicts arise amongst the personnel, being mission-centric diffuses heightened emotion and tension and lifts deflated spirits.

The 3rd Commandment

Thou shall NOT exist in vain.
Thou SHALL prepare for profitability.

I remember the confusion I had around the word "vain" as a child. From an early age attending Catholic school, I had heard it, "Thou shall not take the name of the Lord Your God in vain." I also heard it in the then-popular Carly Simon song, "You're So Vain." The first means "without purpose" and the second "excessively high-opinion of self." My little mind could not handle the juxtaposition of these two uses of the word then, but they both make total sense to me now, as an adult, thinking about the nonprofit arena. Thinking too highly of oneself is pointless, i.e., without purpose.

While the "excessively high-opinion of self" will be discussed in the 5th commandment to honor others, for this 3rd commandment, we'll focus on "without purpose."

Your organization should not exist in vain—without purpose.

We are do-gooders, you say, working to make a difference in the world. Our work is not in vain! Of course, no one wants to exist in vain. But to not exist in vain, it is crucial to consider your mission's actual impact and how you measure it.

Examining the institutional structures upon which the entire charitable contribution tax-deduction paradigm is based, and the various laws and policies making much of the work of nonprofits necessary are beyond this work's scope. However, we can't reflect on whether or not we exist in vain without pausing to consider our relationship to these structures.

You may be thinking, "we're a performing arts organization" or "we're fighting to cure cancer." Or "we have nothing to do with laws and policies. Or you might believe nonprofits have to remain politically neutral and try to stay out of the fray. Not endorsing one political candidate or another to protect our 501c3 status does not mean we can't speak out about the policies, laws, and practices that lead to social problems. During a strategic planning process, don't be afraid to examine your institutional role in confronting, perpetuating, or ignoring systemic inequity.

And in a world where systemic racism and inequity continue to run rampant as an undercurrent throughout society, we cannot discuss the challenge to not exist in vain without questioning how our mission either confronts or perpetuates racism, structural oppression, and institutional inequity.

With the recent tragic deaths of George Floyd and Breonna Taylor, not to mention countless others, many organizations published statements in support of Black Lives and against racism and committed to addressing their relationship to systemic inequities. The demonstrated solidarity, while commendable, is insufficient.

Relationship to Racism, Oppression & Inequity

When my son was in kindergarten, I parked my car in his nonprofit school's parking lot, only to see a man yelling and shouting at someone in another vehicle. I assumed both were parents, but I took note because the man's language was both profane and racist. When the man then entered the school building through a side door, my concern heightened. When I informed the principal of the encounter I'd witnessed, she assured me I must be mistaken because the man in question was the board president. When I assured her of my observation and expressed that no such behavior should be tolerated by anyone, rather than confront the problematic behavior of a board member, the school leadership dismissed it as "impossible."

While you might think this incident doesn't speak to the quality of education in the classroom (although the quality quickly became questionable), it spoke to the tolerance of racism and the lack of integrity within the organization.

When we tolerate racism, we perpetuate it. If we are not anti-racist, we are racist. In this, and every other situation, we must separate ourselves from any racist. We either fight racism, or we perpetuate it.

During a strategic planning process, it is essential to prioritize your growth as an organization committed to undoing the structures perpetuating racism, continued marginalization, and inequity. Every do-gooder must answer, both individually and as an organization: What would an anti-racist organization look like? Do our mission, solution, policy, programs, or practices confront or perpetuate these issues?

Confront

An organization working at the forefront of advocacy is likely confronting systemic inequities rooted in racism and socio-economic oppression. Unfortunately, this is not always the case. Just because you are fighting for a marginalized community's rights doesn't mean you are genuinely confronting the systems causing the marginalization in the first place.

You'll want to ask yourself some fundamental questions: Does our leadership look like those we are fighting for or serving? Do we actively reject the white savior complex which sees People of Color, the disabled, or the poor as less than or victims needing to be fixed or rescued in some way? Do we do for others rather than empowering them to become the heroes of their own stories? Do we listen to hear and understand the community's goals?

And if we don't work directly in service of People of Color, the disabled, or marginalized communities, have we explored why significant portions of the population have been excluded from our community?

At one point, a small private school I worked with needed new exterior doors. In discussing funding options, I suggested she consider looking for grants to support improvements to meet ADA requirements. "We don't have anyone in a wheelchair," she said. To which I replied, "Perhaps that's because you aren't ADA complaint."

At another school, I was pleasantly surprised when a member of the strategic planning committee approached me to discuss how they might increase diversity in their student population, especially since they'd incorporated the concept of diversity into their mission statement. When I offered suggestions for reaching out to the communities of color in the adjacent neighborhoods, she promptly clarified they didn't mean "that kind of diversity." She simply meant she wanted to ensure everyone within their one-mile radius (with $1-2 million homes) could afford to send their children to the school.

So, as you reflect on whether your organization exists in vain, don't forget to ask yourself how inclusive you are. And if you're not, how is your community is so exclusive?

Perpetuate or Ignore

Suppose you believe you can ignore race issues because you "don't deal with those kinds of things," or serve an all-white community, or you're apolitical. In this case, you're perpetuating racism—and other systemic inequities. Don't be this organization. Attend webinars or workshops. Read about the issues. Hire a consultant. Learn what it means to be anti-racist and fight against the white-supremacist, patriarchal systems making any of these three world-views possible.

Impact

In addition to the fundamental question of how your organization addresses systemic inequity issues, we also need to consider other areas of impact and management to ensure we do not exist in vain. Too often, organizations measure impact by the number of people who participate in programs or receive services. While this is one measure of impact, it is not always the most important.

When your mission is to feed and shelter the homeless, counting how many people you feed and shelter is measuring impact. If your mission is to eliminate homelessness in your city, understanding and demonstrating impact is a bit more complicated. Eliminating homelessness is not even as simple as building houses. To eliminate homelessness, you must address the root causes, including lack of affordable housing, unemployment or low wages, domestic violence, and LGBTQ+ teen issues.

You must ask more challenging questions: Have we reduced the number of newly homeless? Have we provided the resources beneficiaries need to ensure stability? Have we tracked the recurrence rate? Have we provided a solution to the symptom without getting to the root cause, or have we offered a remedy for the underlying symptom?

If you provide education, workforce development, or socio-emotional learning programs, how do you measure impact? A school can easily have a 1200-person student body. The number of students says nothing about the students' academic growth, social-emotional learning, ability to achieve academic success at the next grade level, or how prepared they are for life.

How do you know if you have been successful? Do you rely on independent evaluative criteria to measure your success rate? Do you have a standard pre- and post-evaluation procedure? How have you evaluated the difference the program has made in the life of each participant? How have you changed the trajectory of a person's life or the community in which you work? How have you moved the needle of inequity and injustice?

While the impact of programs and services is dependent on both the scope of service and the ultimate vision of the Promised Land, the fundamental question when considering effectiveness is *what difference* participation in a program and service makes—in a beneficiary's life and society as a whole.

> The fundamental question when considering effectiveness is *what difference* program and service participation makes in the beneficiary's life and in society.

The *i grow Chicago* organization works to empower a community on the south side of Chicago. By recognizing the local residents' value, talent, and power, they work across the scope of services to provide critical, crucial, and cultural benefits to residences within their community. Developing a cross-section of services to a hyper-local geographic area means they measure impact in many ways. They count impact as the number of ID cards, job interviews, and jobs secured; the families fed by their community garden; attendees at their afterschool programs; and even the number of hugs exchanged. From a once-abandoned home in a small neighborhood, they create a Promised Land offering hope and change that will reach generations to come. Whether or not *i grow Chicago* leadership has studied asset-based community development, they implement its principles by mobilizing community members to develop their strengths and take ownership in finding solutions to their problems.

If your vision is "an end to the daily walk for water worldwide and the eradication of waterborne illness" (*Clean International*, cleaninternational.org), being able to identify the impact of a program within a local region is critical. Developing the assets the community already possesses will provide credibility and help you more quickly attain the broader vision to go global. When you first focus on a specific geographic region, you can better track and share WHY your mission matters and your solution works. Mobilizing the community, you can build a well to provide clean water in a remote village of Honduras or Uganda. You can demonstrate the impact the well has on individuals at each level of Maslow's hierarchical pyramid of need within the locale, and how a more robust village positively impacts the country and even, ultimately, the world.

Not existing in vain means you continually evaluate your program's effectiveness, quality of service, and professionalism. You must have the best people you can find, doing the best they can do, to have the most significant impact on the problem you are solving for the most people possible. While each organization's situation will be dependent on the industry, the ultimate mission and vision, and the community and culture within which you work, if you are not consistently evaluating your impact and your quality of service, you may be existing in vain.

Who's at Your Table?

When an entrepreneur goes after investors in the start-up world, a primary consideration from the investors' perspective is the leadership team. Many investors want to know each team member's résumés, personality, and attitude and how they operate as a team. Regardless of the product or service's potential, most investors won't invest if the team doesn't meet expectations. Without a group of informed, innovative, and motivated go-getters, the product is bound to fail. Investors are willing to take risks, but they don't want to throw their money away. They want assurance they aren't investing in vain. Donors, particularly high-level donors, are no different. Donors don't merely back a budget; they buy-in to a vision. Who you have at the table is part of the vision.

If you've recently launched your nonprofit, you may have cajoled your friends and family members into joining the board. They helped you meet the minimum requirements for submitting your Articles of Incorporation, obtain licensing, and file your tax-exempt status. They may have agreed to help you jump through the hoops of red tape to get you going. That's all good. But it's rarely a sustainable model unless your family and friends are high-capacity individuals who are 100% ALL-in behind the organization. Many organizations that hit instant stardom and quickly achieve measurable, notable impact do so because of high-powered family members and friends who share their vision. These founders begin at high capacity.

Whether you're the founder, executive director, or board member, you cannot do this alone. For any organization, but even more so for a small or early-stage organization, those with fiduciary responsibility (i.e., your board) must be your core supporters offering time, talent, and treasure. When you have the right people (time and talent) with the right attitude, the money (treasure) will flow, and your capacity will become self-perpetuating. You will attract more of the right people and create a capacity-building culture focused on creating impact.

But don't fret. If your family and friends don't have lots of connections and tons of money, you can still do good. You simply need to be strategic in getting the right people to the table. Who's around the table determines your capacity and potential, and your core community of supporters are those most invested in turning the vision into reality.

Define Roles and Responsibilities

The first step in gathering people to the table is determining what type of board best fits your vision and mission. While the most common, traditional model for nonprofit boards is a governance model, don't ignore the other options out there. For example, a Federally Qualified Health Center (FQHC) is required, by law, to maintain a board composed of 51% consumers of the center itself. Organizations invested in the Asset-Based Community Development model often establish a constituent representative model similar to FQHC. [See "The Innovation Journal: The Public Sector Innovation Journal" Volume 12(3), 207, article 5, for one perspective on various governance models.]

Do you have clients, participants, or beneficiaries of your organization on your board? Do you share the governance with those you make decisions for or about? Although some states may have specific board structure requirements, the IRS in the United States does not stipulate governance or organizational structure. The board's makeup, the number of members, term limits, etc. are left to each organization. The important thing is for your bylaws to clearly articulate the governance model you adhere to, you follow tax laws and ethical principles, and your bylaws and practices align.

Janet Cobb

Welcome Demographic Diversity

The wisdom of any group is far more than the simple sum of the parts. For years, the nonprofit world has been lamenting the lack of diversity in leadership. The lament has only gotten louder and more intense with the uprisings of Summer 2020. Studies have shown the lack of diversity at the highest levels of foundations and organizations and disproportionate funding to nonprofits led by people of color, particularly Black women. Many groups like *Charity So White* (charitysowhite.org) and *Community Centric Fundraising* (communitycentricfundraising.org) have drawn attention to the various ways this lack of diversity in leadership influences the entire industry.

If you are looking to ensure your organization does not exist in vain, be sure to engage individuals of diverse races, gender, sexual orientations, ethnicities, economic status, abilities, and personality traits. Be sure to include individuals from within and from outside your service population.

This diversity is important because people's life experiences inform how they think, react, and relate to others. And when you welcome various perspectives, you will end up with a wide variety of possible solutions and outcomes. By only bringing on people who look, act, and share your experiences, you limit the organization's potential.

In our search for diversity, we need to consider how we define "good fit seriously." We must honor the perspectives and characteristics each person brings to the table. However, we cannot bring diversity into the conversation to silence the very ideas and perspectives the variety might bring, regardless of how challenging and inconvenient the voice.

The truth is, we don't know what we don't know until someone points it out. So, when we welcome diversity, we need to be prepared to be made uncomfortable and challenged to think and act differently. If we remember the mandate to keep the mission as the mantra and make mission-centric decisions, we will understand the value diversity brings to the table.

Create a Skills & Demographics Matrix

Deciding the skills and characteristics needed and defining what you need to do to move the mission forward helps you intentionally build your team. Whether you rely solely on volunteers or you employ paid staff, each person should clearly understand the part they play and be confident they have the skills, temperament, and resources to get it done.

Rarely have I seen an organization flourish when the board languishes. If the board is not engaged in fulfilling its role, your organization will struggle. What is the quality of service of your board? How engaged is each member? Do they understand the distinction between the board's role and their roles as individual members of the board?

Develop the Board

If you don't have the best person or people in place to fill a role, articulate the responsibilities, skillsets, and characteristics needed for optimal effectiveness. You may not find the perfect match immediately but knowing what you're looking for keeps you from settling for second best. You want to keep working on developing the board.

Ultimately, recognizing the difference between your current situation and your desired reality will facilitate conversations with prospective board members, staff, volunteers, and donors that move you from making excuses to finding solutions.

- *Nomination and onboarding*

Finding people with PASSION for the mission—eager, honest, respected, with integrity—is critical. You also need individuals with specific skills to provide the necessary advice and oversight to bring your vision to reality.

Developing a skills and demographics matrix helps you to engineer who sits around the table strategically. By creating a matrix to identify what you are looking for in board members, you can more carefully find members who can fulfill their responsibilities within their area of interest or expertise. Play to people's strengths; recognize and respect what they bring to the table.

Consider which categories of demographics (as shown in the illustration below) are most important to your mission? How will you prioritize? Then examine where you might be able to find those individuals. Consider searching in local Chamber of Commerce directories, meetup groups, nonprofit consulting associations, community banks, university continuing education programs, your church, local business associations. Look for local realtors, lawyers, etc. who might be advertising locally. Check other nonprofit websites in your area to see where their board members are coming from and possibly when their terms will end. You aren't trying to poach any members but knowing someone has served on another board means they may be interested in supporting another when their term ends.

	A	B	C	D	E
1	**Board Skills Matrix**	# of Current Members	Desired # on Board	# of Prospective Members	# still needed
2	**Desired skillsets**				
3	Building and grounds (architect, engineer)				0
4	Community Relations				0
5	Financial: Accounting				0
6	Financial: Auditing, oversight				0
7	Financial: Investing				0
8	Fundraising and Development				0
9	Governance (CEO, ED)				0
10	Human resources				0
11	Law, Legal experience				0
12	Marketing/Communications				0
13	Organizational Management				0
14	Prominent Community Member				0
15	Real Estate Sales				0
16	Real Estate Investment				0
17	Technology				0
18	Other				0
19	Other				0
21	**Personal Style**				
22	Attentive to detail				0
23	Practical 'worker-bee'				0
24	Strategic thinker				0
25	Strong communicator				0
26	Team player				0
27	Visionary				0
29	**Community Affiliations**				
30	Business affiliations				0
31	Corporate relations				0
32	Education				0
33	Philanthropic/ Foundation organizations				0
34	Political influence				0
35	Religious organizations				0
36	Social Media following				0
37	Social services				0
38	Other				0
40	**Resources**				
41	Capacity and interest to solicit others				0
42	Capacity to bring others to give				0
43	Capacity to give				0
45	**Race/Ethnicity**				
46	African American/Black				0
47	Asian/Pacific Islander				0
48	Caucasian				0
49	Hispanic/Latino				0
50	Native American/Indian				0
51	Other				0
53	**Age**				
54	Under 18				0
55	19 – 34				0
56	35 – 50				0
57	51 – 65				0
58	Over 65				0
60	**Gender**				
61	Female				0
62	Male				0
63	Nonbinary				0

- *Formative Development*

Taking time to build interpersonal relationships among board members to understand how different personalities and characteristics inform decision-making goes a long way to building an effective board. I'm not suggesting you have the time or resources to run off to the mountains for a week of team building but taking time to build a community can be time well spent.

With individuals coming from various educational and professional backgrounds to gather at your boardroom table, you want to establish an empowering culture. As part of the onboarding process, or during an annual retreat, you could introduce tools to give everyone a frame of reference and vocabulary to identify different perspectives and approaches to puzzle-solving.

You might consider inviting a facilitator to conduct personality inventories used by many employers, like *CliftonStrengths, Myers-Briggs Type Indicator, the Enneagram, DISC, The Big Five, or the Keirsey Temperament Sorter.* Or you could use even simpler tools like discussing with which character in Winnie-the-Pooh or Star Wars you most identify or which Harry Potter house you belong to, and why? While less formal tools won't provide standardized results, the conversation can provide incredible insight and build community.

Creating opportunities for board members to understand themselves better and getting to know one another on a personal level builds trust and compassion. As board members discover who is at the table with them and how they might view life differently, it opens the door for honest and open communication about personal passions, limitations, and expertise. Taking time to identify different individuals' perspectives and experiences around the table will also break down communication barriers and highlight the value of collective wisdom.

- *Annual Self-assessment*

In addition to establishing and sticking to term limits for every board member, one of the most effective methods for keeping your board fresh and fit to govern is introducing an annual commitment and a self-assessment process. Even well-intentioned people lose their way, so a yearly commitment allows everyone to pay attention to if they walk the walk or if they're all talk.

At the beginning of each year, ask your board members to review their roles and responsibilities and re-commit to them. Allow them to articulate how much time they can offer, what talents they will share, how much support they will either give personally, or be responsible for bringing to the organization. Halfway through the year, provide an opportunity for everyone to evaluate their progress individually and then again as a collective. Encourage them to share their success and to discuss what obstacles they are encountering in their efforts.

Were their eyes bigger than their stomachs when they committed at the beginning of the year? Do they need to adjust their commitment because of a change in life circumstances? Ask board members how you can help them be successful. Do they need training? Would they be more comfortable working in pairs?

Establishing this self-assessment process alleviates some of the tension that arises when board members aren't meeting their commitments. Much like mission-centric discernment discussed in the 2nd Commandment, a standardized self-assessment process keeps it about the mission rather than about personalities. Individuals will begin to see if their actions match their attitudes and whether they can live up to their commitments. By the time the next commitment form needs to be signed, they will better understand how they fit into the matrix of skillset and demographics needed around the table and if they can provide these resources.

A Note on Working Boards

Let's be clear: If the organization is volunteer in nature with no paid employees, board members may be responsible for implementing programs and running events. People like to call this a working board. The board's role is to act collectively to advance the mission and ensure long-term viability through fiscal and operational oversight, with legal and ethical integrity. Members act individually in all other capacities. When board members fill the roles and responsibilities of various program elements, they are volunteers who also serve on the board. In these cases, members must distinguish between acting as an individual who happens to be on the board and acting collectively to make decisions. Retaining the distinction between governance and operations in this way, regardless of governance structure, is critical.

Retaining the distinction between governance and operations is critical.

Prepare for Profitability

As you measure your impact and work to not exist in vain, you can't forget, do-gooder—having nonprofit status is no excuse for not running your mission as a business. And make no mistake - you are in business!

Being a tax-exempt nonprofit is an IRS tax designation, not a business model. Being a nonprofit means no individual can personally withdraw profits from the organization as a distribution for personal gain as owners and stakeholders in a for-profit business can—and should. Once bills are paid, including salary and benefits, all profits remain within the organizational coffers to further the mission and more effectively realize the vision.

You can develop consistent, robust revenue streams and keep money in the bank at the end of the fiscal year. You can charge for services rendered and maintain a reserve or rainy-day fund, and you don't need to pay your employees a pittance. We'll discuss overhead more in the 8th Commandment, but, for now, understand: you don't have to exist in crisis mode, never sure about your cash flow, because you're worried about keeping overhead costs low. Operating in constant crisis mode can be detrimental to the mission and, therefore, contrary to the 2nd and 6th Commandments.

I am suggesting that nonprofits have a responsibility to their stakeholders to be attentive to their profitability. I'm not suggesting you shouldn't put resources into maintaining robust fundraising efforts. But if any department needs to realize a profit (however it is measured), it is the fundraising office. While impact is an important measurement, the fundraising efforts are the for-profit entity of the nonprofit business. Remember, without the money there is no mission.

Profit vs. Profitability

Are you prepared for profitability?

Notice, I asked, "Are you prepared for profitability?" Before we go further, it is essential to distinguish between profit and profitability.

Profit is simply the money left after expenses. A for-profit business's financial objective is to have money left over after conducting business so that shareholders get to put money in their pockets. For a nonprofit organization, the "money left after expenses" is expected to be invested back into the mission.

Profitability is a relative term that considers an organization's efficiency in making a profit relative to its resources. Like "return on investment," profitability in a for-profit entity calculates how much money it takes to raise a dollar.

Distinguishing between profit and profitability is vital because a nonprofit's purpose is not making a profit for shareholders but impacting society. If you make a difference with a few resources, you demonstrate you'll have a more significant impact with more resources. This speaks to your profitability.

The question is, can you articulate for a potential donor how their gift will make an impact? Can you demonstrate how an increase in revenue will not simply be throwing good money after bad to maintain the status quo? Can you ensure their money will make a difference? In other words, what is the return on their investment? The return may not be monetary—it may not increase your profit, but what good will come from it? And what will it cost?

Your job is to show the donor how every penny they spend is well worth it.

Being prepared for profitability means you need to be laser-focused on reaching the next level of excellence. This laser focus often has nothing to do with money. Instead, it means you need to get your entire house in order.

You cannot increase your expense budget simply hoping your income budget will follow suit. I see this all the time. Rather than design the fundraising budget based on the previous year's revenue, many organizations create budgets around their ever-expanding expenditures or arbitrary fundraising percentage increases.

Of course, the more money you have, the more quickly you can acquire additional resources to hire the best talent. When financial resources are limited, the temptation is often for the board to place unreasonable demands on the executive director or director of development and vice versa. Right-sizing financial expectations will reduce this tension and the risk of high staff and board turnover.

Create Diverse Revenue Streams

Another critical element to not existing in vain and being prepared for profitability is positioning your organization for long term viability. Creating diverse revenue streams is one way to enhance viability.

Mike called me for coaching services because 95% of their operating budget came from the family foundation of a friend of the founder. Mike had been hired to work in communications with the hope of raising additional funds. Their founder had never drawn a salary and was nearing retirement. The board of directors' meetings consisted of infrequent and inconsistent phone calls, where the founder shared program updates. The founder knew the legal requirement to have three board members, but the board knew little about the organization. No governance. No strategic plan. No succession plan in place. Even without a background in finance or fundraising, Mike knew this organization was not sustainable. Sure, it existed. But at any moment, if the founder or the funder friend walked away, or worse, died, how would it survive?

A higher-education language enrichment program relied heavily on funds from the Department of Education for 50 years. They reached out to me when the Department suddenly cut their funds. They scrambled desperately to engage the most apparent potential donor base they could: alumni. Having never had a strong alumni relations program, they struggled to build relationships. They had to reduce their programs for several years until they could build up their individual donor fundraising programs.

When you rely too heavily on any specific revenue stream, you run the risk of a budget crunch if anything happens to the resource. We'll discuss how to develop these revenue streams further in Part IV, but for now, let's outline the various streams you should consider to manage your mission better:

- *Earned Revenue*

    Earned revenue could include contracts from partnership organizations, the sale of products directly related to your mission, or fees for service from program participants or clients.

- *Grants*

    Grants can be a boon to the budget but often require a front-end commitment of time, competition for funds, lag time for disbursement of funds, and strict reporting requirements—not to mention the unreliable nature of the funding due to shifting foundation or governmental priorities.

- *Corporate Giving*

    When you consider developing a corporate giving program, remember a corporation might give to an organization for one or more of several reasons.
    - They may be looking for advertising opportunities in front of your audience.
    - They generally agree with your vision and mission and agree to provide monetary support.
    - Their values are your values, and a partnership will further the vision of both institutions.

All that being said, creating corporate relationships relies on building personal relationships within the corporation. Understanding which reason will motivate a gift is critical to how your organization should approach the corporation.

- *Special Events*

    Many organizations rely heavily on holding events to sustain their efforts. They have golf outings, 5Ks, and silent auctions with the hope of creating awareness for their cause and an influx of cash. The concept isn't all flawed. Getting a group of people into one space to learn about and support your mission can be an excellent experience for everyone and provide a quick influx of cash and support. However, events are often labor-intensive with low return on investment, particularly when you factor in labor costs.

- *Individual Giving*

    For the most part, individual giving revenue streams do not have the same limitations as grants, corporations, or special events. As we've discussed throughout, individual fundraising is about building relationships. The individual giving revenue streams usually fall into a few categories: major gifts, annual gifts, monthly gifts, and planned gifts—which ideally are each developed to further the diversity of your revenue streams.

Without robust plans, policies, and diverse revenue streams in place to ensure the long-term viability of the organization, I dare to say, do-gooder, you may exist in vain.

Manage Your Mission

To successfully achieve your vision and fulfill your mission, to avoid mission creep, and to exist with purpose, you need to manage your mission. Remember, a nonprofit is a business. As you make vision and mission-centric decisions to keep the organization on the right path, don't ignore legal, moral, ethical, and managerial best practices.

Whether you're a founder, new executive director, or a volunteer board member, if you don't have a basic understanding of business, surround yourself with those who do. Look for a mentor or coach who's done this before; take a business course or two; ensure the organization has an effective board and a trusted advisory committee to turn to if needed.

Before or while undergoing the strategic planning process, don't neglect the business aspects critical to longevity. Are you in compliance with federal and state regulations regarding board governance, insurance, fundraising, and financial accounting? How often do you review your bylaws to make sure your bylaws and your practice align? Do you have policies and procedures to ensure you aren't person-dependent and your systems will outlast any individual? Have you made an effort to know what you don't know?

- *Quality of Service*

    Like any business, you need to provide high-quality service. This standard of service must reach across every aspect of the organization. Expect quality from the person who answers the phone or greets visitors at the front desk, every program delivery person, and every board member. Don't only expect high quality standards, create policies and procedures to measure those expectations. Do you set clear expectations for professionalism among all your staff and volunteers? What does that mean? Do your expectations honor the differences of those around the table or in the office? Do you have policies and procedures to eliminate confusion and ensure personality or personal agendas don't override policy, particularly when it comes to personnel decisions? Do you provide frequent training and professional development opportunities to ensure your board, staff, and volunteers are aware of and comfortable with best practices in your industry? Do you engage in a formative evaluation process with the board, staff, and volunteers?

- *Money Sense*

You don't need to be a financial genius with an MBA to lead or govern a nonprofit, but you also can't be afraid or ignorant of numbers. If you don't have a basic understanding of budgeting and nonprofit accounting and money management, spend time researching the topics online or at the local library or bookstore, or attend a webinar or workshop to get educated. You don't have to dig into the nitty-gritty of every nonprofit tax law and accounting practice. Still, you also can't shirk your responsibility to operate in a fiscally responsible, ethical manner. While it is important to delegate tasks and not micro-manage professionals, as a board member or executive director, it is your responsibility to maintain oversight of the financial situation. Become familiar with the jargon and processes as quickly as possible. As you bring bookkeepers, accountants, and other financial folks to join your board or leadership team, soak up all the knowledge you can.

- *Human Resources*

    Another critical element of managing your mission is handling the various aspects of human resources. Creating documentation outlining the roles and responsibilities and the policies and procedures regarding expectations of professionalism and confidentiality for the individuals involved in governance and operations is no small task. Yet it is an important one. Whether your personnel is paid staff or volunteers, you need policies in place to protect you and them. Do you correctly display employees' rights and responsibilities under OSHA? Have you written social media, document retention, whistleblower, and other policies? Have you ensured you are correctly handling employee payroll, workers' compensation, benefits packages, unemployment insurance, exempt and non-exempt status? Do you conduct training in the area of sexual harassment and race discrimination?

- *Risk Management*

    Having worked in Catholic schools for a long time, I'm well aware of the importance of protecting children from dangerous pedophiles. Imagine my surprise and concern when a client who enlists volunteers to serve children in overnight shelters NEVER requires background checks! As someone who holds a ServSafe Food Management certification (like in the restaurant industry), I'm flabbergasted when those who prepare and serve food under various conditions aren't expected to take food sanitation classes. Yes, I know, do-gooder, you want to trust the dedicated volunteers who are offering their time and talent for the good of your mission. Truth is, without the proper portfolio of insurance and without following common industry operating standards from the for-profit sector, you run the risk of ending up in dire straits.

To not exist in vain and to prepare for profitability, don't forget to manage your mission.

Promised Land

Creating A Strategic Plan

A strategic plan is a tool to move your organization from reactive to proactive mode. Through the planning process, your stakeholders focus on the desired vision and confirm the mission by establishing long-term goals and a short-term action plan to achieve those goals. Together, you envision, design, and create the future.

A robust strategic planning process can stimulate creativity and new approaches to long-standing concerns; clarify critical values and beliefs that can more easily be articulated to new employees, volunteers, and donors; and provide a framework for day-to-day decisions.

Foundations and many savvy donors research an organization before donating. They want to understand your purpose and plan of action. The plan and its implementation become a blueprint for your organization's growth and become an excellent public relations piece shared with potential funders. More importantly, the strategic planning process prepares you to communicate and fundraise effectively.

Dust-Collector or Change-Driver

In the early stages or in smaller shops where one or two individuals do everything, the thought of stopping to plan your work might seem laughable. You may have heard the saying, "Plan your work and work your plan."

But who has the time? You're putting out fires, managing operations, and running on the hamster wheel. Your time and energy are spent. And speaking of spent, you have no money, right? What good is a plan if you don't have the money to make it happen?

You spend most of your time reacting. An effective strategic planning process stimulates proactive visioning. You confirm your vision of the Promised Land. You clarify values, spark creativity, and build consensus. You design intentional growth and change. Your strategic plan exposes potential holes in your solution, irons out wrinkles in your process, and prepares the organization for profitability.

Articulating long and short-term goals for the organization also protects the organization from becoming too person dependent. Everyone involved walks away with goals supported by objectives, which you'll achieve by taking specific actions to deliver measurable outcomes. Everyone in the governance and operations of the organization has agreed upon and is aware of them. Your vision can become a reality regardless of who sits in which spot in the rowboat. Remember the fictional donor who asked the four officers about their top priority and searched high and low until she found an organization where everyone gave the same answer? Unanimity is made possible with a strategic plan.

Process

The process for strategic planning will depend on your organization's size and complexity, years in operation and lifecycle stage, number of program participants, engagement of donors, and your relationship to the larger community.

A volunteer, board-driven organization focused on raising funds for programs in another country might limit their outreach to the handful of volunteers who regularly engage in fundraising. A private secondary school that has served a community for 75 years might ask for input from alumni, former or current parents, students, teachers, and board members. They could also reach out to local elementary feeder schools or the admissions directors at colleges to which their students regularly apply. A performing arts organization could ask for input from current and former actors, audience members, donors, and community members.

The more participants in the process, the more insight you'll gain. That said, design the format to ensure any negative feedback does not override the presentation of positive feedback—or vice versa. Encourage participants to think about what factors will impact possibilities for the future they envision. The strategic plan isn't about looking back to point fingers or assign blame, but is, instead, an opportunity to understand where you are right now and how you got there so you can now clarify where you want to go and how you'll get there. Reviewing impact and establishing priorities rooted in reality and current capacity ensures prospective donors and board members, employees, and volunteers can create positive change, growth, and impact.

Step 1. Gather Input

Ideally, a comprehensive planning process involves looking at the big picture and the fine details. Gathering input from various sources and through different formats creates a complete picture of how organizational stakeholders perceive and are impacted by your policy, procedure, and programs. How people feel about your organization is as critical as your impact reports and financial information. Broad strokes provided by anecdotal narrative offers a perspective to complement data-driven evidence. Using various methods to understand your current reality opens your organization to future possibilities.

Of course, objective facilitators, third-party agents, and online tools provide a sense of safety and removes the fear of hurt feelings the anonymity allows: the more anonymity, the more honesty.

- *Broad Strokes Approach*

  Conduct a comprehensive gathering of information from stakeholders through snail mail, e-mail, online, or phone surveys. The broader the scope of input, the better the perspective you gain. Ask participants to answer both binary and open-ended questions or write personal narratives about their relationship to and experiences with the organization.

- *Systematic Focus Group*

  Invite key stakeholders to participate in focus groups or one-on-one interviews. Conducting face-to-face conversations helps to understand a participant's intentions and emotions, which writing may not readily convey. Focus groups allow for asking clarifying questions, avoiding misunderstandings, encouraging participation, and creating the possibility for feedback that might trigger a meaningful memory of a shared experience.

- *Intensive Deep Dive*

  Gathering key stakeholders into one room at one time (for a few hours or over days) for a deep-dive, focused conversation can be intense but effective. Intentionally carving out time to schedule strategic planning acknowledges the importance of the process and demonstrates a commitment to improvement and growth. For some organizations, this deep-dive step is the first and only approach to gathering input. Sometimes it is the last step of the information gathering process conducted by the board and leadership.

Step 2. Analyze

Once you've determined who and how you will be gathering information and input, it is crucial to decide which information you want to collect and what method(s) you will employ to analyze the data. The questions you ask and the framework you use is essential to facilitating the conversation. While SWOT is one of the most common analysis methods, you can choose between several forms or employ a combination of techniques to ensure you've captured the most pertinent information and have enough insight to create a bold vision for moving forward.

Generally, whichever method you use, you'll want to reflect on what realities, trends, and possibilities are happening both within your organization (strengths and weaknesses) and outside of your organization (opportunities and threats). From there, you'll formulate optional responses and articulate your aspirations for the future—as outlined in the methods below.

The temptation is often to start from the point of weakness or threat to focus on fixing or improving what is wrong from a reactionary standpoint. Looking at weaknesses and threats is often a reactive process which, while allowing for vision, can feel like you are trying to prove something to someone. The foundation for a positive, productive planning process begins with a celebration of your strengths and taking advantage of present opportunities to build more robust, more impactful solutions, which involve proactive visioning.

- *SWOT*
  - Strengths – Where do we excel? What makes us proud? What makes us unique?
  - Weaknesses – Where do we struggle? What do we not do so well? Where can we improve?
  - Opportunities – What is happening in the community that could support our mission delivery?
  - Threats – What is happening in the community that could make our mission delivery more difficult?

- *SOAR*
  - Strengths – Where do we excel? What makes us proud? What makes us unique?
  - Opportunities – What community and market trends align with our strengths? What partnerships could lead to tremendous success?
  - Aspirations – What do we care deeply about? What do we want to achieve in the future? How can we make a difference?
  - Results – What measures will determine our success? How do we tangibly track our success?

- *PESTLE*
  - Political – Are there any recent or pending changes in government policy that will impact our mission?
  - Economic – Will trends in economic growth impact the disposable income of beneficiaries and prospective donors? How will these trends affect the demand for programs?

- Social – Will current social movements impact our beneficiaries, mission delivery, or vision?
- Technological – Are any tech developments (device types, software development) likely to impact the need for our services or our mission delivery?
- Ethical – What data handling practices and regulations, environmental considerations or other ethical considerations do we need to consider when planning for mission delivery?
- Legislative – Are any new laws on the horizon that could affect program and mission delivery or the need for our services?

- *SCORE*
  - Strengths – Where do we excel? What makes us proud? What makes us unique?
  - Challenges – Where do we struggle? What do we not do so well? Where can we improve?
  - Options – What options do we have for responding to the various insights we've gained? How can we respond?
  - Responses – Of the many options we have, how will we choose to respond?
  - Effectiveness – What measures will determine our effectiveness? How do we tangibly track our success?

- *Handling Inaccuracies*

During a recent strategic planning process with a client, one survey respondent expressed a concern that the program's geographic scope was too limited. They believed so strongly in the program model that they wanted to see the organization spread further across the region. The respondent, a volunteer at the organization, did not realize it was one of many affiliates of a national program. The ONE mission was to serve within a narrow geographic scope, knowing others have established affiliates elsewhere.

Some organizations will cite the fear of these inaccurate responses as justification for narrowing the number of individuals asked to provide input. When these types of misunderstandings creep into the responses, the temptation is to ignore them as outliers. When my client realized even a key stakeholder held misperceptions, they took note. They recognized the need for more clarity in messaging around their relationship to the national organization moving forward. The inaccuracies and outliers that surface in surveys and research empowers otherwise underheard voices and offers insight into critical misperceptions you may need to address.

Step 3. Establish Focus Area Goals

In my experience facilitating strategic planning through this analysis process, areas of aspiration and concern begin to emerge, and themes become evident.

Any policies, procedures, or programs that strengthen your mission should be explored for reiteration, expansion, and next level of excellence as much as those identified as weak or troublesome. The question becomes, "How will we get closer to the Promised Land?" Once you've envisioned the future for those you serve, you will begin to formalize aspirations and state the goals that will help you realize your vision.

In the earliest stages of strategic planning, as you establish focus areas and create goals, you want to avoid the limitations imposed by financial concerns. Remember that your ONE mission, not money, must drive your plan.

If I had a dime for every time someone challenged this approach by questioning the point of creating goals and vision for change when they "have no money," I'd be a gazillionaire. Yes, some elements of your plan will require financial or personnel resources, but if you allow your current reality to dictate your goals for the future, it will be tough to envision anything new. In creating your vision, you create the story that will compel others to embrace it.

Ask yourself, "In five years, what do we want our reality to be in this focus area?" State your goals in the present tense. Think of what your desired state of being will be.

Last spring, I met with a client in a Chicago suburb who, for many years, has offered shelter to the homeless on nights when the temperature falls below 20 degrees. During this strategy session, many members felt strongly that shelter should be available every night of the winter, regardless of the weather. Others were concerned they simply could not afford the expense. Their ONE mission is to serve people who are hungry and homeless. The shelter is integral to their service definition, but they rely on local faith communities to provide space. After a good deal of discussion, they decided to include daily overnight shelter in winter months as one of their 3-5-year goals. The next step would be to be deliberate in planning how they would make it happen. They researched cost, consulted with the faith communities providing the venues, determined paid and volunteer personnel needs, and created the messaging for why it was critical and its impact. They estimated that, with concerted effort, they would meet their goal in three years. And they did, although not quite in the way they anticipated.

Step 4. Determine Objectives and Actions Steps

A goal without a plan is simply an idea, a hope, or a dream. Without specific objectives and action steps to realize your goals, you are not likely to achieve them.

In the example above, the organization articulated the need to research the cost and the logistics of making it happen. They wanted to communicate clearly with supporters that nightly winter shelter was a priority. They understood raising funds could take time, but they now had a specific fundraising goal.

By the time winter hit, their research was complete, and a few local businesses had agreed to sponsor revenue-sharing events to support the cause. Unfortunately, a homeless person died in the early winter cold. Local media outlets brought attention to the problem, and a church community stepped forward to offer a large donation. While the circumstances leading to the nightly shelter being made available were tragic, the organization had prepared the cost and logistical resources needed to make nightly shelter available. Within days, they solved the problem. During the historically cold winter of 2018-2019, homeless individuals in town had shelter available every night.

Without taking the bold step of declaring their vision and the action steps needed to get there effectively and efficiently, providing nightly shelter could have taken many more months, if not years, to become a reality.

Remember, as the Roman philosopher Seneca is said to have said, "Luck is where preparation and opportunity meet." Don't leave your mission and vision to "luck."

Step 5. Articulate Measurable Deliverables and Due Dates

A measurable deliverable is a document, product, event, or action to be completed by a specific, predetermined date. These deliverables act as mini-goals to help you accomplish your action steps and objectives. As any life coach will tell you, setting SMART goals that are specific (S), measurable (M), attainable (A), realistic (R), and time-limited (T) is one of the first steps in reaching your potential.

The same holds for a strategic plan. The strategic plan is not a set of vague ideas collecting dust on a shelf. Instead, it becomes a list of actionable steps you can identify as either on hold, in progress, or complete. For example, suppose your objective is to "research" something. The deliverable could be for a specific person is responsible to "submit a report of the research results" to a particular person or group by a designated date. Without determining the implementation portion of your strategic plan, you walk away from the process with big ideas that are likely to sit on a shelf collecting dust rather than being realized.

Step 6. Assign Responsibility

Nonprofits are notorious for killing every idea by committee rather than empowering individuals to make decisions within their responsibility scope. By distinguishing between the different roles involved in each action step, you eliminate delay and empower individuals at varying levels of the organization to take ownership for moving the objective forward.

While various project management methods exist, my default method is the RACI Process, which articulates who is responsible (R), accountable (A), consulted (C), and informed (I) during implementation. Using this method, you can articulate the relationship between the various individuals participating in the process.

- *Responsible (R)*

    Which volunteer, staff, or board member will spend time, energy, and talent to complete the deliverable by the due date? Do they know? Do they have the time and talent to get it done correctly, without being micro-managed?

- *Accountable (A)*

    If the responsible person doesn't complete the action, will anyone else be held accountable? Is the accountable person able to step in to complete the task promptly, if needed? Particularly, if the responsible person is not the executive director or a board member, to whom does the responsible person report?

- *Consulted (C)*

    Does anyone need to be consulted during the completion of the action step? Who has the experience or expertise to support the responsible person so they aren't working in isolation, baring the entire burden for the action step? Are those being consulted aware of their role in getting this done? Can they commit to the time it will take to offer input in the timeframe needed to meet the deadline?

- *Informed (I)*

    Not every board member and staff person needs to be involved in completing an action step or meeting an objective. Having "too many cooks in the kitchen" leads to unnecessary delays and micro-managing. Clarifying who will be kept informed of the progress of a deliverable or action step gives the person responsible more ownership of the project. Establishing this RACI process is an essential step to providing a sense of ownership to the community and creating a pipeline of potential future leaders in the organization.

Step 7. Report Progress

A good deal of time and energy goes into any strategic planning process. For this reason alone, you need to hold yourselves accountable for following through on the plan. With the best intentions to meet your goals, if you don't have a simple method for updating progress, your strategic plan will become a dust collector.

Creating a visual indication of progress to be reported at pre-determined intervals (weekly, monthly or quarterly) will allow leadership to maintain oversight without micro-managing and be proactive if any critical action steps are in danger of not being met. With this type of reporting, you can address concerns before they become problematic to the overarching goals for the strategic plan.

When you have a strategic plan in place to genuinely drive your actions, everyone in the organization, from the boardroom to every office and throughout every program, knows the priority and works towards it. With clearly articulated goals and action steps to reach them, everyone is in the same boat, rowing in the same direction.

A strategic plan demonstrates to key stakeholders and potential supporters that you've taken the time to openly and honestly assess your current reality, and you've detailed how you will navigate reaching your goal. With this strategic plan in place, you can tell the story of your WHY, the problem you are addressing, and how you plan to enter the Promised Land efficiently and effectively.

Then, when the donor walks in asking about your priorities, you'll all know exactly how to respond to receive the million-dollar check.

Part II: The 4th Commandment

"When the well runs dry, we know the worth of water."

Ben Franklin

When The Well Runs Dry: The Currency Of Water. https://www.forbes.com/sites/ashoka/2014/09/12/when-the-well-runs-dry-the-currency-of-water/

Promised Land

The 4th Commandment

Thou SHALL keep holy the Sabbath.
Thou shall NOT burnout.

Okay, do-gooder, it's time to take a breather.

By now, if you followed Commandments 1-3, you've focused inward: you've defined your Promised Land, identified your mission, and tested your solution and impact. The first three commandments concentrated on getting your vision, mission, and goals aligned, establishing priorities, and creating your roadmap to the Promised Land.

Before we jump into the public phase of communicating our vision, mission, and strategic plan with the world, let's pause for just a moment.

Do-gooders aren't alone in allowing our passion and hope to drive us, forgoing any semblance of work/life balance, but when our goal is to save the world, even our little corner of the world, our work can feel like it's never done. We will always be busy.

Despite the many years laborers have fought to have a 40-hour workweek and to establish and observe national holidays, nowadays, being busy is considered noble. We wear it as a badge of honor. Somehow, we've turned the dignity of work and providing for our families into our identities and sense of self-worth.

Don't give in to the myth!

Despite what thought-leaders, commercials, and social media memes shout at us from all directions, success in life (or even reward in death) doesn't depend on consistently accomplishing five (or 7 or 10) things before breakfast and reading ten (or 12 or 30) books a year or rising at 4 am to begin your day. The drive to be uber-successful is not the answer. Wearing busyness as a badge of honor is foolish.

In a society very much focused on getting things done, I find wisdom in the 4th commandment to "Keep Holy the Sabbath." The concept of keeping holy the Sabbath is rooted in one of the Judeo-Christian Genesis creation stories where, on the 7th day, God rested. Or, as the Q'uran would say, "When the call for the Friday Prayer is made, hasten to the remembrance of God and leave off your business." Whether you or your organization is faith-based, faith-driven, or secular, I caution you not to ignore the importance of this 4th Commandment.

Moving your mission forward is a marathon, and perhaps a relay, but not a sprint.

At some point, we must leave off our business to rest. Or, in more secular, modern-day terminology—we can't forget to practice self-care.

Whether you reserve a specific day each week, time of day, days of a month, or weeks of a year isn't the issue. Taking time out to refresh, regroup, relax and rejoice in all life has to offer gives us the energy to return to our ONE mission, ready to do what it takes to get to the Promised Land.

"But I love what I do!" you say. I hear you. I do. I love what I do, too.

When our work is our passion, and we live and breathe for the cause we care about, work and personal life often become entwined.

As the saying goes, "Do what you love, and you'll never work a day in your life." (According to Quote Investigator, the origins of this saying are dubious.) Taking action (posting to social media, shooting off an email, sharing your vision with someone over coffee) becomes as much a part of your day as brushing your teeth or your morning cup of coffee. We don't feel stressed or overwhelmed because it is more who we ARE than what we DO. That's not necessarily a bad thing. I hope every do-gooder on the planet enjoys their work.

Even then, any simple internet search will offer scientific evidence that physical and mental relaxation is good for both body and soul. You cannot run at full speed for too long. You will burn out. What good does that do you or your ONE mission?

You aren't wrong to work towards accomplishing your vision, especially since this mission is often not for you; it is for others! After all, your drive to keep pushing, over-extending, and taking pride in your busyness stems from your vision. Once you have a fully-functioning, high-powered program funded by major donors, grants, and crowdfunding campaigns have gone viral, you'll rest, right?

No one should fault you; you're doing a good thing, right?

You're a do-gooder—a hero, a martyr for the cause. Just think of all the warm wishes and kind words that will be shared in your wake and your obituary when you collapse from exhaustion. Remember, bringing your vision to reality and helping others meet their physiological, psychological, and self-fulfillment needs doesn't happen overnight or by running yourself ragged.

The problem for so many small and early-stage nonprofits is they have so much to do and too few resources to do it. Well-meaning do-gooders who DO take the time they need to rejuvenate can end up feeling guilty or embarrassed. In some cases, this causes division and hard feelings among those who don't. This dynamic isn't good for anybody.

And do-gooders, we can't leave the search for balance and the practice of wellness only to the individual by encouraging self-care. Using terms like "self-care" instead of creating an organizational approach to wellness puts an added burden on the individual to figure it out for themselves. Then they must be courageous enough to go against the grain of selfless dedication to the mission to ask for what they need. Instead, let's focus on creating a culture of wellness and encourage practices to reduce the risk of burnout and disillusionment.

Work SMART not HARD

The 4th Commandment reminds us to reject the myth that we can get it all done if we just work harder.

I always told my high school students that it's better to work smart than hard.

Too often, I hear do-gooders lamenting that they, their board, staff, or volunteers, "just need to work harder." After all, the only way to get things done is to have people who work harder, right?

Wrong. Many do-gooders and organizations work hard, no doubt.

But hardworking leadership often bumbles into board development, hiring, program development, and fundraising in a hurried (H), anxious (A), relentless (R), and sometimes desperate (D) manner.

Don't Work Hard

- *Hurried (H)*

  How often do we rush into something, only to realize we weren't ready to execute correctly? We hurried, but our lack of planning, attention to detail, and preparation led to mistakes and failure.

- *Anxious (A)*

  If we act impulsively, without setting realistic, not goals allowing us to focus on one step at a time, we feel overwhelmed by the enormity of the task at hand. We haven't broken down the tasks into an actionable, achievable timeline. We haven't lined up the talent to get the job done right. Anxiety sets in, and we become less effective.

- *Relentless (R)*

  Being relentless is not always negative, but sometimes we relentlessly pursue our passion while ignoring our beneficiaries' or donors' hopes, desires, and goals. We can come off as impatient and aggressive.

- *Desperate (D)*

  Unlike someone calmly and systematically pursuing articulated goals, the desperate person or organization works in fits and starts, hopes for magic money, and comes across as unfocused, unorganized, and unprofessional. Desperation is palpable.

Working HARD ignores the importance of articulating the talent and skills needed to make mission-centric decisions, which minimizes the risk of burnout. Working HARD zaps effort and energy and rarely leads to finding or mobilizing talent for your organization.

Work Smart

Working SMART, on the other hand, involves a more holistic approach to problem-solving and progress. Unlike the more familiar SMART goals, working SMART means creating a sustainable (S), meaningful (M), aware (A), rightsized (R), and thankful (T) approach to everything your organization does.* [I adopt the SMART acronym used here from blogger Kathy Gottberg at Smart Living 365, www.smartliving365.com.] Unlike SMART goals focused on setting and achieving goals, working SMART is more about adopting an attitude towards your work and your life.

- *Sustainable (S)*

    When you make decisions for yourself and your organization, do you explore how sustainable the program, approach, policy, etc. will be as time passes?

- *Meaningful (M)*

    How meaningful to the vision and mission is what you are doing? Does it move the needle? How important is it? How will it influence the impact of your work?

- *Aware (A)*

    Are you doing it because you've always done it? Because someone expects it of you? Out of habit? Or are you intentional in the decisions you make and how you spend your time?

- *Rightsized (R)*

    We'll discuss rightsizing a bit more in the next section, but for now, remember working SMART involves not trying to do too much in too short a time.

- *Thankful (T)*

    Reminding ourselves to have a thankful attitude in our planning and work is essential to avoiding burnout. Being thankful reminds us it isn't all about us and our work is more significant than ourselves. [See more on gratitude in the 5th Commandment.]

Right-Size Your Expectations

Whether you are in the early stages of mission development or your organization has been around a while, rightsizing your expectations around resources of time, talent, and treasure (i.e., money) is fundamental to long-range viability and accomplishing your mission. With adequate time, talent, and treasure, you can achieve everything; you accomplish nothing without them.

To create a culture where everyone keeps holy the Sabbath (however this is defined), those within leadership must determine how much time, talent, and treasure they can personally commit to the fulfillment of the mission— and encourage others to do the same.

Then when you plan, you already have the parameters for realizing the plan's success. By articulating and honoring each person's commitment of time, talent, and treasure, you can plan from within limits imposed by your current reality and will, therefore, be more likely to be successful in reaching your goals.

Respect Time: 240 Days-a-Year to Move the Needle

Everyone has 24-hours in a day and 365 days in a year (except leap year, then you gain an additional 24-hours). Yes, we have laws regulating paid time off. Still, we all know many people who work well beyond the hours they're paid for—not to mention the tireless dedication of volunteers who often offer their time and talent beyond their regular work responsibilities. Allowing for weekends, holidays, and annual vacation—the times built-in by law and common practice, at the very most, you realistically have 240 days-a-year to make progress in fulfilling your mission; 240 days to move the needle and to accomplish your goals.

I now proclaim: we should reserve every leap year's extra day for recreation and repose.

If you have full-time paid employees, base all goals on this reality. With 8 hours per day, each full-time employee has 1920 hours a year to accomplish everything on their work-hours *to-do* list. If you are working with part-time paid staff, they only have a portion of the total. And if you rely solely on volunteers to accomplish your mission, you should count on far less available time, not to mention variations when they offer their time.

Yes, someone might <u>choose</u> to work beyond those hours, but to honor the commandment to keep holy the Sabbath, I'd urge organizational leadership to discourage this practice. It would be wise to review the federal and state labor laws regulating the hours and circumstances under which an exempt and non-exempt employee can work or offer to volunteer. Let's not exploit the goodwill and good nature of our colleagues.

More than just regulating hours, creating a wellness culture could include practices focused on stress reduction and relaxation and respecting boundaries and personal differences.

Respect Boundaries and Personal Differences

Whether paid or volunteer, everyone has the right, even a duty, to set boundaries others respect. Among paid employees, not to mention volunteers, not everyone's boundaries will be the same. When working with a diverse group of individuals, they will each have personal commitments that dictate their availability and determine how they will prioritize time spent on moving the mission forward.

Family obligations, work commitments, and personality traits will influence when their allotted time is available. While one person might need to check and send organization-related emails only on weekends, at midnight, or strictly during office hours, this doesn't mean others should do the same. Do not expect anyone to stay late, work all weekend, or be available 24/7—or at the whim of a zealous founder.

Asking everyone to complete a commitment form outlining their capacity and boundaries goes a long way to right-sizing expectations around how much time the organization has, in any given year, to move the needle and get to the Promised Land.

Remember, if as the executive director, program director, or staff member, you are hired to work part-time, be wary of putting in extra hours "to get it done." The organization does not need to acquire additional resources if you keep going the extra mile. If you complete 30 hours of work but only clock 20 hours, they do not need to increase your hours because you'll give it to them for free. And when you move on from the organization and need to replace your position, they will not clearly understand the resources required. The board and leadership team should know what it takes to get the job done.

Even when you love what you do, allowing the organization to exploit your passion causes you harm and is detrimental to the organization's long-term viability. Suppose the passionate do-gooder who goes above and beyond normative hours leaves for any reason. In that case, the organization does not likely have the wherewithal to continue operating at the same level of effectiveness and efficiency because they've relied too heavily on one person's zealousness.

Act Quickly But Not in a Hurry

Being realistic about the resources you have prevents you from acting in a hurry but motivates you to act quickly. Even though the temptation to hurry is most prominent at the early stages of running a nonprofit, any organization that has not right-sized their expectations around their resources of time and talent is in danger of acting in a hurry.

When you haven't taken the time to plan, you run the risk of continually reacting, especially when a financial crunch hits. The danger of being reactive rather than proactive because you are in a hurry is that you run the risk of turning away potential board members, volunteers, and donors, being completely ignored, or getting what I call go-away money.

Go-away money is the small gift given by someone who could provide much more, hoping it appeases you and you go away. Someone who can donate $25,000 gives you a check for $2500 because you rush into an ask before doing your homework and building a healthy relationship.

Acting quickly, on the other hand, means you respond promptly, effectively, and efficiently. If you are implementing the three-plan approach to mission development I advocate for here, you realize getting from point A to point Z requires planning and time. By adopting the three-plan approach, you understand that implementing the appropriate plan is better than risking never reaching your goal.

Practice Wellness

Early in my fundraising career, a keynote speaker at a conference said, "If you're not hearing "no" two to three times a week, you aren't asking enough."

Fact: If you're raising money, you'll hear "no."

When we're heading to the Promised Land, the journey can feel excruciatingly slow—like forty years of wandering in the desert. If you are fundraising to support this journey, it can feel even longer and more grueling. We don't quickly see the results from the hours of work needed to raise awareness, cultivate a relationship, secure a gift, and thank donors.

Clients will sometimes ask if anything helps besides a glass of wine. As a teetotaler, I've had to find other ways than alcohol to handle the seemingly endless marathon, but I certainly appreciate the sentiment.

Besides treating myself to the not infrequent brownie, cake, or box of dark chocolates at the end of a long day (yes, I meant box, not piece), I encourage myself and my clients to find sanity-saver activities, especially those providing a clear sense of progress.

Sanity-savers

The president of a school where I worked made it his responsibility to physically walk out to the corner of the property to change the black plastic letters on the events sign. The entire process took about 15 minutes, but it got him out of the office, into fresh and sometimes freezing air, and offered a change of scenery and perspective. A sports-loving principal I knew grabbed a dust mop to clean the basketball court when she needed a thought-break. One of my personal sanity-saver favorites is buffing floors. I love feeling the machine twisting at my waist as I guide the machine along the floor with my hips and seeing the shiny wax left behind when I've finished.

Find a sanity-saving activity that can provide a much-needed break and lets you see progress during your workday. When you're feeling like you've accomplished little to nothing because your cultivation and stewardship hasn't yet reaped results, seeing progress in something you enjoy can boost your ego and comfort your soul.

And from an organizational perspective, try not to judge the little quirks you might see in another who may be engaging in a sanity-saving moment when you think they're just wasting time.

Hobby or Project

I also recommend having a hobby or long-term project you enjoy in your free time outside of the office. You could paint a room, do jigsaw puzzles, crochet or knit, sew, build a cabinet, fix a car, repair a boat. Find something just for you, or perhaps something you can enjoy with a loved one, which doesn't require deadlines but shows clear progress.

And if you spend a good deal of time sitting at a desk or generally indoors, finding physical activities that bring you joy can be a lifesaver. As someone who does not enjoy routine, I've developed various activities to get me moving: biking, walking, and gardening, to name a few.

I can't even fathom how those working from home with small children during the COVID-19 are managing, so please forgive me if this all sounds ridiculously oversimplified. But I highly recommend integrating household chores into your workday. As one who sits on video calls most of my day, I've found tasks like changing laundry, cleaning a toilet or sink, and taking out the trash to be great reasons to get up and move around. Not to mention drinking water consistently. That sure makes you get up regularly!

Most of all, as you're discovering new ways to practice wellness, try to avoid too many rules or regulations so your sanity-saver, hobby, movement, or relaxation tricks don't become burdensome responsibilities.

Consider Your Circumstances

Building and running a business takes hours, months, years of dedicated, consuming hard work. So many do-gooders, like entrepreneurs, have big ideas—and big hearts. Unfortunately, big ideas and big hearts aren't always enough on the journey of starting-up or running a business or organization.

Personal Capacity

While we've all heard the rags to riches stories of homeless people turned entrepreneur making millions or a nonprofit's cause going viral overnight, this isn't the norm.

At more than one point in my life, I've had a vision for solving one problem or another. The most elaborate idea developed about ten years ago. I noticed that in many Chicago neighborhood laundromats, small children rolled around in chairs or on the floor for hours waiting for their parents to wash, dry, fold, and pack up bushels of laundry. My inner teacher voice shouted, "This isn't fair! These kids don't have a chance! Where are their enrichment opportunities other kids have?"

My mind instantly jumped to full-blown solutions, incorporating holistic wrap-around services for the entire family, filled with workout rooms, kitchens, tutoring services, and enrichment programs. I went all-in researching vacant buildings and sales of the needed equipment. I could envision an oasis where families could reserve a home-away-from-home, so Saturdays weren't wasted merely waiting for laundry. I had discovered my solution and wanted to make it happen!

While immersing myself in all things startup and business-related, I quickly realized I wasn't personally ready. I had three school-aged children, my husband was in graduate school, we'd been hard-hit financially by the 2008 recession, and I'd been struggling with depression. After considering my capacity to take on such a massive project, I set it aside because I knew, at the moment, my health and my family had to come first. I might be able to pull off some semblance of a program, but the mission would suffer, and so would me and my family.

I've worked with more than one founder who, like me, had a very clear vision of what they wanted to do. Big picture thinkers with big hearts see the perfect solution, clear as day. More than one has envisioned complex multi-million-dollar solutions without first understanding or working with those negatively impacted by the problem they thought existed. They hadn't done their market research, identified community assets, clarified their mission, or tested their solution with a minimum viable product.

I caution them to take stock of their capacity to manage the business and program side of their mission before leaving their personal Egypt to wander the desert in search of the Promised Land.

Financial Stability

You've heard the saying, "Don't quit your day job," usually directed at struggling artists and writers who aren't likely to strike it rich overnight. But you can say the same for nonprofit founders. Only quit your day job to start a nonprofit if you have another income source, a trust, or a savings fund.

Many do-gooders begin with visions of saving animals, teaching children, empowering girls, supporting cancer patients—believing they will raise enough money to make a living. If you're starting from scratch to launch a nonprofit, plan on volunteering your time and talent, and even your treasure, long before you can draw a salary. Starting a nonprofit because you can't find a job or want to be your own boss is not always a viable or good idea.

Launching a nonprofit is often a full-time job but won't provide a full-time paycheck any time soon.

Serving the mission and fundraising for the mission when you are worried about putting food on your table can kill your dreams for changing the world. If you don't have a personal revenue stream, consider finding one before launching a nonprofit.

Emotional State

As a leader (paid or volunteer), your state of mind and emotions often dictate, or at least heavily impact, the organization's culture and climate. You want to ensure you can handle the pressure of leading an organization before you jump in and bring others along with you.

I've worked with many clients who experienced a traumatic event, which inspired them to launch a nonprofit, so no one would ever have to go through what they just did. While I understand their motivation, sometimes the pain is too raw. The emotion drives them, but when they face the details and tediousness of budgets, operations, personnel, and fundraising, they get overwhelmed and lose heart.

Handling family situations and managing emotional crises doesn't preclude you from launching a nonprofit. These can be a driving force. But realize what you're getting into before you part the Red Sea for others to follow while you barely survive.

Sense of Humor

Urgency and anger can be powerful motivators for action, but if everything in life is super serious, do-gooder, leading a nonprofit could destroy you. Be careful not to tank your mission before you get anywhere near the Promised Land.

Having a sense of humor means you don't take yourself or life so seriously that you can't find joy, irony, and ludicrousness amidst the struggles. Can you laugh? Can you laugh at yourself? You don't need to be a standup comic or continuously joking around, but can you search for differing perspectives in troubling situations over which you have no control?

Desire for Control

One of the most challenging aspects of leading a nonprofit, particularly for a founder, is a desire to control how the vision and mission unfold.

Of course, none of us want to think of ourselves as control freaks, myself included.

I like to think I'm laid back and easy going. And I'm certainly open to new ideas and ways to get things done. I learned when I moved into the administration that I expected everyone to share my vision and work ethic to achieve that vision. My passion quickly turned into a need for control when I realized the mission (and my livelihood) depended on others' work ethic, attitudes, and abilities. I quickly concluded, not only do I never want to have a boss, but I also never want to be a boss.

If you think that as a nonprofit founder or executive director, you'll be your own boss, you're mistaken. And if you believe everyone who works at a nonprofit organization shares the same motivation and work ethic, you've got another thing coming. The vision may be your baby, and you may be super excited to get to the Promised Land, but don't forget you aren't alone on the journey—

and sometimes this means things don't go your way or as quickly and smoothly as you'd hope. And, yes, as a founder or executive director, you may have a good deal of autonomy, but you aren't your own boss; you answer to the board of directors, to your donors, and to the trust of the community you serve.

Part III: Communications: Commandments 5 – 7

"The single biggest problem in communication is the illusion that it has taken place."

George Bernard Shaw

"Wit & Wisdom." The Week, no. 1042, Dennis Publishing Ltd., Oct. 2015, p. 23.

You've identified the problem, the vision, and the solution in a way that prepares your organization for profitability. Your strategic plan has become your roadmap for moving from your current reality to your Promised Land. You've taken a good, hard look at the resources everyone brings to the table, personally and as an organization, and you've incorporated boundaries and self-care into the fabric of your expectations.

Now, you're ready to invite others to join you on the journey. You're ready to find others who care about what you care about. You're ready to build a community. And to build a community, you will need to build relationships. And to build a relationship, you must communicate.

As any relationship expert worth their salt would tell you, communication isn't just about talking. You've also got to listen actively. You want to create a dialogue, not a monologue.

Sometimes communication has nothing to do with words but relies on observation and action. Through our actions, we convey respect, dignity, hope, loyalty, gratitude, and so many more emotions—emotions that are the foundation for a lasting relationship.

In the next three commandments, we will explore the tools for communicating your mission, vision, and strategic plan to keep your community engaged so your fundraising flourishes.

The 5th Commandment

Thou SHALL honor everyone.
Thou shall NOT brag about yourself.

New on the job at a private school, I called an alum who'd given $2500 gifts for two years but had stopped a year before my arrival. Hesitant to meet with me, he finally agreed to see me at his office when I promised to take only 15 minutes of his time. When I arrived, he offered me a seat as he reached into his drawer and pulled out an invoice. He placed it squarely between us on the desk. "I never received a thank you. I heard nothing about the student for whom I provided the scholarship. Never received a word from anyone about what is happening at the school. Then I got an invoice!" I glanced down to see an invoice with $2500 listed as the *amount due*.

The 5th Commandment calls us to honor our father and mother, "that your days may be long, and that it may go well with you in the land that the Lord your God is giving you" (Deuteronomy 5:16).

As we reach out to communicate the vision, we are called to honor everyone: those we serve, our volunteers, staff, and donors. Too often, we brag about ourselves, our great work, our programs. The 5th commandment reminds us not to make our organization the center of attention.

Thank You

Thank you—two magic words we were taught as children can make or break a friendship. The same is true of the relationship between an organization and its donors.

Assuming you have some semblance of a cordial relationship with your parents (and believe me, I am not saying you SHOULD), you know the importance of wishing them well on their birthdays and Mothers' and Fathers' Day.

Similarly, *most* nonprofit leaders know the importance of sending a tax receipt after someone donates. You dutifully thank donors for their gifts, informing them all donations are tax-deductible to the full extent of the law. You might even add your handwritten signature on a snail mail piece as a personal touch or inform the donor of the great work you're doing.

Hopefully, this transactional exchange is the least you do.

Then what? Given how busy we all are, many of us move on to the next task and hope the donor gives the next time we ask. Our thanks must be more than transactional to truly build a strong donor base and secure long-term support for our mission. Communicate with donors between your appeals for money. Don't be the organization that waits to say, "Thanks, now give again."

And indeed, don't be the invoice organization!

Instead, create a culture of gratitude across the organization so each community member, board member, staff, and the smallest, newest donor alike feels it.

Create a Culture of Gratitude

For a long time, I wrote about and encouraged *an attitude of gratitude*. While it has a nice ring to it, with time, I've honestly become convinced this cliché could do more harm than good. Attitudes can be fleeting and flexible. The word *attitude* conjures in my mind the hands-on-the-hips caricature of a fickle teenage smart-aleck who smiles and plays nice when they want something. We need more than an attitude, which can change without notice—we need a culture of gratitude.

Culture runs deep and informs policy, procedure, and practice. Organizational culture permeates the daily existence of volunteers, staff, board members, and even program participants. Culture is the voice of the person who answers the phone, the greeting at the door, the comments overheard in the hallway.

The role of an organizational leader is to create a culture of gratitude.

You can ensure gratitude permeates your culture by first cultivating and encouraging daily expressions of gratitude—during program delivery, in one-on-ones, and at meetings.

What culture exists within your organization around gossip, spreading rumors, and back-biting? What is the atmosphere or tone within your organization? Are relationships rooted in honest communication and respect or passive-aggressive machinations? How are board members talked about when they aren't in the room? What is the relationship between leadership and staff? How are

---

The role of an organizational leader is to create a culture of gratitude.

---

your beneficiaries treated, spoken about, and spoken to? Do you listen to the rumors about others? Do you allow personal politics to get in the way of mission-centric and donor-centric decision-making?

A culture of gratitude may not put an end to the whispered meetings after the meeting—you know, those meetings of two or three folks, offline, complaining and criticizing everything that happened in the larger group meeting. A culture of gratitude could, however, change the content of such discussions because it will curtail the sense of exclusion, dissatisfaction, and disengagement simmering just under the surface in many organizations.

As a leader, do you show your appreciation for the little things board members, staff, and volunteers do? Or are the privileges and gifts you experience through the course of a day taken for granted? Do you take time to be grateful, just because? Is your office atmosphere one of negativity, disappointment, and pessimism? Do you empower others or deflate them? Does anyone leave a meeting or program with you feeling unappreciated?

Gratitude Policy

A gratitude policy is an all-encompassing, documented process for how the organization demonstrates appreciation for the board, leadership, staff, volunteers, donors, and program beneficiaries. A gratitude policy articulates the particulars for creating a gratitude culture that will lift spirits and encourage collaboration.

A gratitude policy is the documented process an organization uses to build a relationship with key stakeholders. The gratitude policy ensures each stakeholder group is thanked in various ways and multiple times throughout the year. Establishing a written policy is vital to ensuring the culture of gratitude is intentional and permeates the organization regardless of who sits in the board room or janitor's closet.

Even more important than writing down your gratitude policy, like the strategic plan, this policy should not be something gathering dust on a shelf. Remember to introduce, revisit, and implement the policy during the onboarding process and regularly throughout the year. Try some of these tips for creating a culture of appreciation and gratitude:

- Express gratitude for the community you serve. How are your beneficiaries talked to and talked about?

- Thank your staff. Recognize the varied gifts staff members bring as key supporters of your organization. Don't take them for granted. Honor and appreciate them.

- Thank your board and other volunteers. Designate months, weeks, or days to honor different members of various groups. Remind them they make a difference.

- At board meetings, prepare thank you cards with notes about each donor and ask board members to write or sign the cards. Better yet, make phone calls thanking donors before the meeting officially begins.

- Be *specific* with praise. General expressions of thanks aren't as useful as expressions making it clear the person doing the thanking knows *exactly* what's worthy of praise. People appreciate the recognition that's specific to what they did.

- Distribute a weekly *Gratitude Report* with a list of donors and volunteers to every staff and board member, so donors' and volunteers' names become familiar.

- Those who receive services from your organization can also be included in creating a culture of gratitude. Don't forget to include service recipients (clients, students, and patients) in the thank you process. Ask them to write thank you notes, make a thank you video or share testimonials about the difference the mission has made in their lives.

- Brainstorm ways to make sure EVERY donor and volunteer knows their gifts of time, talent, and treasure matter.

- Mention volunteers and donors on the website, in newsletters, in social media posts. Get the word out: Your staff, volunteers, and donors are FANTASTIC!

- Find opportunities to thank donors when they least expect it. An unexpected token of appreciation goes a long way in creating a connection with a donor.

Remember, if your donor holds the organization in higher esteem than the organization holds the donor, your culture of gratitude is broken and needs to be fixed.

Sample Content for Gratitude Policy				
Gift Level	Gift type	Method	Timeframe	Responsible Party
☐ over $10K	☐ Check	☐ Phone call	☐ Within 6	☐ Board
☐ $5000 -	☐ Cash	☐ Video	hours	Chair/ED
$10K	☐ Online	Message	☐ Within	☐ ED
☐ $1000 -	☐ In-Kind	☐ Text Message	24 hours	☐ Director of
$5k	☐ Stocks	☐ Handwritten	☐ Within	Development
☐ $250-	☐ Annuity	Note	three	☐ Board
$1000		☐ Form letter	days	Member
☐ Under		receipt	☐ Within	☐ Program
$250		☐ Email	one	Officer
☐ Monthly		☐ Token of	month	☐ Program
gift – any		appreciation	☐ 3-month	Participant
amount		☐ Recognition	mark	
☐ First-time		event	☐ 6-month	
gift – any			mark	
amount			☐ 9-month	
			mark	

Gift Acknowledgment Policy

A gift acknowledgment policy is a written policy focusing on the donor relationship's transactional elements by articulating what happens when a donor makes a gift. To create and foster gratitude that will have your donors feel appreciated and your board members excited about fundraising, you will need to develop a donor-centric gift acknowledgment policy. A win-win for any organization!

What happens from the moment a gift arrives? Is the speed of acknowledgment determined by the size of the gift? Who is thanking? What is the thanking method? Are major gift donors thanked more quickly than lower-level donors? Is a $10K gift acknowledged the same way as a $10 gift? Does the $10 gift donor know their donation is appreciated? How often are acknowledgment letters sent? Each day, each Friday, when ten gifts have come in, or every so often when you can make time? Is a letter the only way you acknowledge a contribution?

Your answers to these questions may vary, and there is no absolute right or wrong answer, but you must do your best to acknowledge all gifts as quickly as possible. Most authorities on donor cultivation will say it is best to acknowledge contributions, whether online or off, within 24 to 48 hours.

Your organizational capacity and donation rates will determine how you handle the logistics. Putting a policy in writing will ensure it becomes an organizational process, rather than being person dependent. Documenting how you acknowledge different gifts provides a consistent operation if someone is on vacation or leaves the organization.

The thank you and the tax receipt are not the same. The thank-you process is relational, and the gift acknowledgment policy is transactional. Once you've sent a receipt with the proper legal jargon about tax exemptions to the extent of the law, stewardship begins.

- *Surprise Your Donors*

One of my favorite mottos is "Thank them when they least expect it." Everyone expects a donation receipt with a perfunctory thank you, at the very least. (Not an invoice!) Doesn't it feel good to be appreciated and thanked unexpectedly?

Your gift acknowledgment policy helps to guide how you can surprise your donors with an unexpected show of appreciation. No, standardizing a practice does not eliminate the opportunity for an authentic and genuine expression of gratitude. The method of regularly expressing gratitude will increase a sense of gratitude for you, your beneficiaries, and your benefactors. Remember, the element of surprise is for the donor, not you.

You can thank donors when they least expect it by developing ways to surprise them. Decide on several thanks-4-giving campaigns per year for various segments of your donor base. You don't have to thank everyone at the same time. When you segment your efforts, you can better manage your time and expense. More importantly, having ongoing thanks-4-giving campaigns involving your board and staff cultivates the culture of gratitude critical to honoring everyone in your orbit.

Creating different ways to thank different groups of donors at various times strengthens your culture of gratitude by keeping it at the forefront year-round without completely taxing your capacity. Consider segmenting your donor groups based on lifetime giving levels, zip code, which program they give to, their birthday month, or the first letter of their last name.

You can take advantage of celebrations like Valentine's Day and Thanksgiving or the organization's anniversary or national theme day/week/month. Seasonal themes like Back-to-School or the first day of Spring could be appropriate. A personal message on the donor's birthday or just because it is the first Tuesday of the month. Hold a gratitude phone-a-thon, or an annual breakfast, picnic, or a simple event hosted by the board. The key is to thank the donor when they least expect it.

You don't need a professional videographer to create a quick-and-easy video highlighting programs and thanking donors for support. A simple phone camera can do the trick, or you can explore software options to make sending videos and voice recordings easy and inexpensive. Sincerity is more important than expert technical precision when saying thanks.

Post social media shout-outs on a daily/weekly/monthly basis. You could even draw names from a weekly lottery. From social media posts to phone calls, emails, letters, and appreciation events, encouraging a culture of gratitude within your organization will make your donors excited to give again, allowing your mission not just to survive but to thrive.

- *Know Your Donors*

At one high school, I identified an alumnus who had given $125 every year for almost twenty years. With a little research, I discovered he was a medical doctor who lived about an hour from campus. I called to ask if I could take one 20-minute patient slot to meet with him during my listening tour, where I wanted to hear from as many alums as I could within my first year. When I thanked him for his ongoing support and asked why he gave with such dedication, the doctor told his story. His father had died when he was a sophomore, and the father's club had paid his remaining tuition for his sophomore, junior, and senior years. His annual $125 gift was his way to give back. I then shared the story of a student whose mother had recently passed and asked if he would offer additional support for this student. With tears in his eyes, he pledged $10,000 on the spot and thanked me. He hugged me and added, "No one has ever asked."

Knowing who your donors are is vital to building the relationships critical to your fundraising efforts, which we'll discuss later. For now, I think it is important to note this donor had been expressing *his gratitude* for the support he received through his annual $125 gift. Because the school had never taken the time to understand his motivation and show appreciation for his support, they missed out on an opportunity to bring joy to both him and the student who would benefit from his increased generosity.

If you're a small shop and fundraising is only one of your hundreds of responsibilities, how do you take the time to know your donors and build relationships?

Begin with a small list, perhaps the top 10 or 10% of donors. Get to know everything you can about them (without being stalky). Learn your donor base; know the names, the numbers, and their reasons for giving. How do they know you? What do they do for a living? Do they have a family? What makes them tick? What do they care about? Why do they give to you rather than some other organization?

Can you visit your donors or invite them to coffee? When you engage with them, listen to their stories as much as you share the organization's news with them. Don't allow the relationship to be one-sided. Understand their interests beyond your organization. If they mention a child's birthday, drop a card in the mail. If their favorite sports team wins a game, shoot a quick congratulations. Let them know you care.

As your organization grows, you may not know every donor personally, but understanding what makes your donors tick is fundamental to developing your culture of gratitude. The more you work on these relationships, the more invested in your organization your donors will become.

- *Ask advice*

A wealthy board member had been the primary donor to her alma mater for almost ten years, often bailing them out when they couldn't make their budget. She loved the mission but was tired of being treated like an ATM when they continually made poor financial decisions. When she learned the staff had secretly moved forward with a major capital project against the entire board's advice and budget approval policy, putting the organization in a precarious financial position, she resigned and vowed never to give another penny.

Two years later, as the new executive director, I diligently worked to repair the relationship and valued the expertise she brought to the table. After seeking her advice on two critical community outreach opportunities, the donor pledged to match all new donations for one year.

Along with growing new donor engagement, I focused on rightsizing what had become a bloated budget. I presented a clear vision for mission-centric program growth aligned with the donor's personal mission in a fiscally efficient way. As I wrapped up the "State of the School" presentation, to which I had invited her and other key stakeholders, seven months into my tenure, this donor who'd sworn never to give another penny wrote a $250,000 check on the spot. This donor matched all new gifts for the year and wrote an unrestricted gift on the spot.

Some executive directors and board members fear that if you ask a donor's advice, the major contributors will butt-in where they don't belong, trying to dictate program decisions and wielding undue influence. Remember: donors, volunteers, and staff are critical to the organization's existence and, therefore, should be involved in envisioning its future.

Asking advice doesn't mean donors make the decisions or jeopardize organizational integrity. When you value donors' opinions and invite them into conversations around program development and expansion, you'll learn what motivates them. You'll also allow for the opportunity for them to put their money behind the ideas they generate or promote.

They don't dictate your organizational direction, but when you better understand what motivates and drives your donors, implementing their ideas becomes a win-win. In other words, if they've shared their vision and making it a reality aligns with the strategic plan and mission-centric decisions, then they are more likely to back up their advice with the money needed to make it happen. As an old saying in fundraising circles goes, *"Ask for money, and you get advice. Ask for advice, and you'll get money."* I like to add, *"Maybe twice."*

- *Build institutional history*

Ok, do-gooder. Knowledge of your donor base will grow with time. As you build relationships, be sure to develop your institutional history. Take good notes and create donor profiles. Whether you're the founder, board member, or database manager for your organization, plan for the day you will not be around to explain the history and relationship of a given donor.

You can keep notes and profiles the old-fashioned way with pen and paper, or in a simple Google Doc, the cloud, or a computer-based donor management system. I know one seasoned fundraising professional who has raised millions for several institutions over the years, who keeps donor notes in packs and stacks of 30 index cards bound by a rubber band on the corner of his desk. The method for building the profile is not so important as the content you are gathering—although I must admit, plenty of fantastic, reasonably priced donor management systems exist.

Whether you are the founder, a new executive director, a board member, or staff, you have a responsibility to ensure the organization's long-term viability. Since donors are one part of any nonprofit's lifeblood, you don't want to lose them.

Consider investing in the technology that helps you track and communicate with your donors—and use it. Start with the free services until you can afford something more robust. Once you have software tools, you can better understand larger segments of your donor population. Who always opens your emails? Who never does? Who likes or shares your social media posts? Who attends all your events? And who brings their friends?

Creating a robust donor profile and understanding your donors is critical to building your culture of gratitude and honoring your supporters, not to mention securing your fiscal viability.

Gift Acceptance Policy

Conventional wisdom might say, "Never look a gift horse in the mouth."

Some nonprofit leaders are hesitant to refuse a gift of any kind. They don't want to pass up a chance to bring in money. The process of creating a Gift Acceptance Policy can help to identify core values and new strategies and clarify—not all sources of money align with your mission.

A board member at a small-town literacy organization I coached suggested holding a fundraiser at a local chain restaurant known for its outspoken political views. Another member believed it best to avoid associating with such a polarizing business that promoted values contradictory to those held by some board members, even though the organization could use the money.

Some organizations proactively reject a donation to avoid being associated with a particular person, business, or ideology. And I'm sure we've all heard stories in recent years of institutions returning major gifts because of a donor's scandal.

You may have heard the recent stories of the young Girl Scout who sold cookies in front of a legally operated marijuana dispensary. While they were happy to take the money she collected, several organization leaders resisted rewarding her sales record because the place she sold her cookies violated their organization's principles.

Cultivating gratitude enables you to identify those moments when an offered gift does not appropriately align with your mission, and when you would do better to reject a gift.

For some organizations, the parameters for accepting or rejecting gifts seem apparent. For example, many private schools have a policy of not accepting sponsorship dollars from drug, tobacco, and firearm companies. Not all issues are as clear cut. Articulating the types of gifts and sponsorships your organization will accept is essential to staying focused on your one mission and vision. The policy allows you to say "no" to any gift that would demand you begin a new program or service that isn't a current focus, even if it aligns with the mission.

If you have articulated your core values, these can often be the guiding factor in determining a gift acceptance policy. For example, if one of your core values is diversity or inclusivity, it would be essential to expect your supporters' shared values. If they publicly reflect exclusionary attitudes, they might not be the best choice for developing a partnership.

This acceptance policy could also outline how you'll handle bequests, annuities, and other planned gifts. Do you have processes in place for the transfer of stocks or other investments? Do you have a formal planned giving program or a legacy society indicating how you steward these donors? Are cash gifts recognized in the same way as in-kind donations?

- *In-Kind Donations*

Another concern of the gift acceptance policy would be in-kind donations. Under what conditions would you accept tangible items like expensive works of art, automobiles, equipment, furniture, antiques, jewelry, property, and real estate? Do you reject all such gifts because of the burden of protecting them or managing their sale? Do you require or recommend an appraisal from an outside, independent consultant? What stipulations should you include about preservation or sales before accepting such a gift? What is the monetary threshold for such gifts? Who has the authority to accept in-kind donations of substantial value?

We can argue the merits of each of these cases but only the written policy matters when it comes down to it. The more clearly you can articulate the circumstances under which you will or will not accept monetary or in-kind donations, the more quickly you can resolve issues. If you don't have a written policy, who has the authority to decide? What criteria do you use to make these decisions? Putting this policy in writing from the beginning will help to avoid discussions that could get too personal and, therefore, messy. In a world where many individuals pay close attention to how corporations and organizations spend their dollars, outlining your policy can't hurt. You may protect critical relationships in the long run. If the policy is written, you avoid personality conflicts and hurt feelings among colleagues and friends, not to mention a hit to your reputation if someone is upset by your rejection of a gift.

Honor Your Team

Be Collegial

Creating a collaborative, collegial environment breeds mutual respect and support. Remember, you don't need to become friends because you sit on the same board or work in the same organization but being respectful, collegial, and considerate for the sake of the mission is essential.

When you befriend one another, you try to see things from one another's perspective, not just your own. You equip everyone with the tools they need to promote the mission. You ask others what you can do to make their job or their participation more sustainable.

The board, as a collective body, is the employer of the executive director. While the board's relationship needs to be open and transparent, the executive director and board members don't need to be friends. Muddying the waters between board and staff with friendship can destroy both the nonprofit and the friendship.

On the other hand, setting a collegial tone will go a long way towards board members and staff supporting you and one another as well. Effective relationships can boost morale, improve retention, and increase engagement in fundraising.

Inform and Update

Some executive directors try to keep bad news from board members and staff. Not a good idea. They aren't the enemy. If a problem is keeping you up at night or you're exploring exciting new programs, others may be able to offer insight.

Between meetings, keep board members and staff abreast of what's happening in the day-to-day operations, about programs and their impact, or regarding any significant changes, so they aren't caught off guard if they hear of it elsewhere. You don't want those most invested in your mission to be surprised in casual conversation with outsiders who seem to know more about the organization than they do. Board members and staff should never be the last to know—whether good news or bad. If you forthrightly offer information, your leadership and management skills can shine, and you position yourself to demonstrate grit and resilience when you hit rough financial or operational situations.

That said, keeping your board informed or consulting them for advice is not the same as allowing them to micro-manage operations. Managing your board is about nurturing a consistent relationship between meetings so the members are confident you can handle the minutiae while they focus on the big picture vision.

Don't Bore Me to Death

Any discussion on honoring your team would be incomplete without acknowledging that board and operations meetings can be deadly if not done right.

Before you start thinking you need to memorize Robert's Rules of Order, consider that these rules were initially published in the late 1800s to transfer parliamentary procedures to non-legislative bodies. No law says your organization must follow them! You might consider researching the 2004 alternative, *Roberta's Rules of Order* by Alice Collier Cochran, or you could make up an entirely new set of rules. You set the tone for conducting your business.

Ask yourself a few simple questions to determine if you need to revamp meetings:

Do board members and staff dread your meetings? Do you spend hours printing, collating, and distributing reports and documents before each meeting, only to review them piece by piece during the session? Does everyone leave the meeting zapped of energy and feeling like they've wasted 90 minutes of their lives? Or God forbid, do your meetings run longer than 90 minutes? Are your meetings backward-looking or forward-thinking? Do you spend meetings picking apart day-to-day operations, staffing concerns, and fundraising events rather than engaging in big picture thinking or long-range vision and planning?

Consent Agenda

If you take advantage of technology, you can conduct a good deal of the perfunctory elements of business offline using a "consent agenda." A consent agenda includes routine items like approval of minutes, adoption of non-controversial policy items, and the presentation of standard financial or fundraising reports. Reports read offline before meetings can become the springboard for discussion, training, and discernment rather than consuming most of the meeting time. Ideally, a consent agenda is distributed days before a meeting to allow members to review and submit questions or discuss concerns. If no discussion is needed, the entire agenda can be approved as a unit item at the beginning of the meeting to save everyone's time and sanity.

Meetings then become a time to question assumptions, like "why have we always done it that way?" and hold probing, robust discussions around crucial strategic, organizational policy and practice. Meetings can become brainstorming sessions about innovative ways to solve the puzzles you address, explore mission growth, and collaborate with other organizations for a more significant impact.

You want board members and staff fired up and eager, not remembering their obligation to your mission as an afterthought. Even the word obligation conjures a sense of duty rather than a passion and love for what you do. Find ways to educate, inspire, and empower your board and staff to be ambassadors rather than overlords or minions perfunctorily performing their duties.

Don't Reject the Naysayer

We've all been in meetings or served on committees with a naysayer, the nitpicker, the Eeyore. We want to ignore them, resist their opinions, or remove them as quickly as possible so we can move forward. Don't they realize we have a world to save!

The naysayers and nitpickers aren't necessarily bad news for a nonprofit organization. Many of the Eeyore's among us have good hearts. They may think saving the world is tough, and they can see all the pitfalls before we can, but they want to get to the Promised Land, too. After all, the naysayers remind us Rome wasn't built in a day, nothing comes easy, and reward carries risk. They deserve to be heard because they help us be better prepared to handle issues we might otherwise not have anticipated.

Rather than dismissing them, consider three simple steps to help you reap the benefits of the naysaying nitpickers.

- *Absorb the friction*

    If you have enough enthusiasm and vision to balance the devil's advocate's hesitation and opinions, the naysayer can help you avoid catastrophe. When the resident nitpicker chimes in to shoot down each new idea with what might go wrong or why it won't work, or has a negative attitude in general, don't ignore them. By acknowledging their perspective as valid, you let them know you're listening and their voice will be heard. Maybe, then, they won't feel the need to jump on an idea so quickly. That said, be sure you have enough big-picture, "yay-sayers" to cushion the blow.

- *Offer equal time*

    Suppose you have established a culture allowing and encouraging equal time for all members to voice opinions. In this case, the perpetual critic's negativity or hesitation won't lead to immediate deflation or abandonment of the idea on the table. Instead, it will be heard as one view among many. Consider asking these individuals to speak in the middle of the conversation, not at the beginning or very end. By allowing the naysayer to voice concerns, you allow for equitable, respectful consideration of everyone's ideas without letting negativity from one become the overriding atmosphere. Indeed, you could begin to rely on these folks to identify the possible pitfalls. Honor their perspectives and world view and allow, even encourage them to offer this valuable contribution.

- *Focus on solutions*

    Hearing concerns or criticism from an otherwise positive person may be easier than hearing the same points from one who always seems to be complaining. But allowing anyone to offer point-blank problems without presenting a positive comment and proposing an alternative approach limits the entire team's creativity and problem-solving capacity. Again, if we consider problems to be puzzles, we want to invite and encourage everyone to identify the pieces needed to solve the puzzle. The entire team benefits when we create a culture of solution-focused conversation.

Implementing these three techniques will ultimately create a culture of positivity and honor, which welcomes constructive criticism and a collaborative, respectful approach to discernment without putting undue pressure on the individual whose mind quickly jumps to the possible pitfalls of any new idea.

When the Writing is on the Wall

In my experience, two significant warning signs of issues between an organization and an individual board member, employee, volunteer, or donor are aggression, and worse yet, apathy.

Does the individual believe there is more wrong than right with the organization? Do they disrespect other board members? Do they breach confidentiality? Do others dread their presence at meetings or events? Are they vocal, in public, about their dissatisfaction? Does a board member, volunteer, or employee shirk responsibility and need to be persuaded to participate, even at the level they agreed to?

Do they ignore efforts to engage via email, phone, and meetings? Do they forget about events or simply refuse to attend?

Keeping an aggressive or apathetic person in the organization at any level can be toxic. Implementing formative development and self-assessment tools will help you to avoid these circumstances. Sometimes honoring the team demands someone (preferably the board president for board members and the executive director for all staff) take drastic steps, speak up and bring an end to the relationship sooner rather than later.

Don't Brag

Have you ever had lunch with a friend who never stopped talking about themselves?

A few months ago, I realized "Narcissa," whom I'd considered a friend, did just that. Each time we got together, she shared story after story about her life and why she knew more than those around her. When I first noticed, I thought maybe it was a fluke. The last time we got together, I took closer note. During our two hours together, I barely spoke, and never once did she initiate interest in what was happening in my life.

Of course, we all lend a listening hear when a friend is in need or simply needs a sounding board from time to time. But, if every time you get together, the conversation (and the universe) seems to revolve around them, you might begin to wonder. You can't get a word in edgewise, and you aren't sure your presence is even noticed or appreciated.

Many organizations try to entice donors by talking about all their excellent programs. They throw out statistics, making sure those who visit their website, read their emails, or see their social media posts know how credible and reliable they are and how deserving they are of money. Demonstrating your solutions are effective and reporting positive impact is important, but it does little to honor your community.

When you brag too much about your organization, you risk sounding like Narcissa.

You also run the risk of your communications reading like a nutrition label. Think about it. The quickest way for a chocaholic like me to resist the brightly packaged candy lining the checkout counter is to read the ingredients and nutrition label. As indecipherable chemicals and daily recommended allowance numbers pop out at me, my cravings and impulse to buy quickly vanish. I realize a momentary bit of joy isn't worth the calories and treadmill time to burn it off.

Donating is often an impulse buy. When your communications read like a nutrition label, you impede the impulse. Instead of describing what you've done, invite donors into what still needs to be done, and how the world will change if they get involved.

The 6th Commandment

Thou shall NOT kill.
Thou SHALL foster a growth mindset.

Many moons ago, when I was a boisterous, passionate sister-in-training (think Maria from *The Sound of Music*), one elder sister repeatedly criticized me. I talked too loudly, laughed too often, didn't eat enough or overate, was too idealistic. The list of criticisms went on. With each admonition, my spirits sagged—until one day, another sister leaned in and whispered, "Don't change, grow."

This line has stuck with me as I trekked through my own life's deserts. As I learned how to grow into myself, I've adopted the world view that there are many ways to do life and every situation offers an opportunity for growth through the power of choice.

Adopting a growth mindset and embracing the power of choice challenges two of the most common death sentences I hear from nonprofit leadership: "We've always done it this way" and "We've never done it that way."

Avoiding growth and revitalization is organizational suicide.

Your board, whether they fully grasp it or not, has power. Your board has the power to breathe life into your mission or to kill it. Without a strong board of directors, your nonprofit will struggle to thrive—regardless of your mission. While very few people join a board or take a leadership role with the intention to kill the organization, if they resist change, they could be dangerous.

At the same time, key leaders within the organization, like the executive director, program officers, and fundraising professionals, hold similar power. How each staff person interacts with beneficiaries and benefactors can also negatively impact your sustainability. If your organizational culture is stagnant and defeatist, viewing every challenge from an attitude of scarcity, you've written your death sentence.

Of course, you don't need to be continuously in a state of flux, changing just for the heck of it, either.

Solid policy, practice, and procedure create consistent service quality, mission integrity, and brand recognition. And a great deal of value comes from tradition. As the saying goes, "If it ain't broke, don't fix it." Don't change for the sake of change.

But if something is broken, fix it! If something could be better, nurture its growth! If it isn't perfect, keep trying!

Like any living, breathing organism, your community must be nurtured and cultivated to bring forth fruit. Ensuring that each person embraces a growth mindset will go a long way to not killing your nonprofit.

Cultivate a Growth Mindset

Every Monday morning, the fundraising staff at one high school gathered to discuss five stories they would distribute as press releases to local publications that week. John, the executive director, knew not every story would be published. He also knew that some might be. Other executive directors, principals, and coaches teased him about having dirt on someone because he received so much publicity.

The fact is, many of the captioned photos they sent each week became filler material for the media outlet when they needed a quick story. Still, it offered the organization free exposure to promote its mission. John knew that for his school to thrive, he needed constant exposure that would be seen by alumni, potential parents and students, and the neighboring communities. He understood that communicating wasn't a one and done task or an afterthought. He put it front and center—and the results were noticeable.

Nurturing a growth mindset isn't a pie-in-the-sky dream that riches will simply manifest to solve all your problems, that every press release you send will garner media attention, or that your email open rate will hit 100%. A growth mindset means understanding and believing that your present reality, whether it be the problem you're trying to solve or the resources you currently have available to solve it, can shift. A growth mindset instills a sense of courage and persistence rooted in the belief that you can accomplish your mission and reach your goals.

A growth mindset instills a sense of courage and persistence rooted in the belief that your mission can be accomplished, and your goals can be reached.

Problem vs. Puzzle

I know we've talked a lot about solving problems, but I like to think of a growth mindset as approaching challenges as a puzzle rather than a problem. The word "puzzle" has a more positive connotation than "problem" because puzzles are usually solvable. When we face a puzzle, we expect a solution exists and simply need to figure it out. The word "problem" can often trigger a defeatist, anxious response that hinders creativity. Calling something a puzzle doesn't make discovering solutions quick or easy, but it can inspire the perseverance, grit, and resilience critical to a growth mindset.

Perseverance, Grit, and Resilience

Even when you begin with a passion for turning your vision into reality, you will still need to rely on perseverance, grit, and resilience to get it done. *Perseverance* keeps you pushing towards your goals for as long as it takes to achieve them. *Grit* is the dogged determination and intestinal fortitude to overcome every obstacle and let nothing bring you down. *Resilience* is the adaptability and flexibility that pushes you to get back up when something has knocked you down—to try again after failure and make another choice.

Don't forget, do-gooder: Large, booming, well-known organizations didn't get that way because they never struggled to raise money or improve their model. Very few organizations achieve overnight success. The Red Cross, United Way, St. Jude Children's Hospital, Susan G. Komen, Charity: Water, and other national and international nonprofit organizations began with an idea and limited resources. They grew through a persistent focus on ONE mission and vision, consistently expanding their capacity by making mission-centric decisions. These organizations live a growth mindset with grit and resilience. They don't give up. They persevere. They know that believing in their vision doesn't mean they don't have to work hard to make it happen. They stay the course and adapt, as needed, always moving closer to the Promised Land.

Capacity and Creative Tension

I know do-gooder. Right now, you're probably thinking, "Wait a minute, you keep saying we need to right-size expectations and to work within our capacity. Now you say to think big and beyond the current reality. What gives?"

The fact is, you have to function within your current reality, but you can't let go of the bigger, brighter vision. Through your strategic planning process, you decided what steps are needed to achieve your next level of excellence. Adopting a growth mindset will act as a driving force to get you there. For this, you'll need to be honest about your current reality AND create a clear enough picture of your vision that people will want to join you along the way.

Find Community

In designing your communications plan, you're working from a growth mindset with the belief that people outside your organization believe in what you do. Your job is to continue sharing your story.

But remember, do-gooder, you aren't trying to convert people to believe in your vision and mission. You're trying to inspire those who already share your values. You're in search of people who care about what you care about. You aren't trying to convince, cajole, coerce.

While it may be impossible to personally build a relationship with everyone, understanding the spheres of influence determined by your community, your people, and your audience will help you to define your message and create your collateral materials.

- *Community*

    Your *community* consists of the stakeholders in your mission who already actively engage and support the work you do. Hopefully, you've already begun building relationships with your *community*. You start with your family, friends, and those directly impacted by the issues you're solving. *Community* members respond to the problem and your solution; they want to make a difference. You enlist them to be board members, staff, volunteers, and donors; they give with their time, talent, and treasure. Your *community* acts on behalf of your mission. They are your key stakeholders.

- *People*

    Just beyond your community are your *people*, on the sidelines watching. They've heard your message, and they care. They share the same types of social media posts, petitions, and articles that you do; they may attend or promote your events or care about your solution and what impact you're having. They are involved in similar efforts to solve problems around the same issue. They might even be in your contacts, receive and open your e-newsletters and follow you directly on social media. Your *people* listen, share, and care about the same things you do, but for some reason, they are not yet fully engaged with their time, talent, and treasure for your organization.

- *Audience*

     Let's suppose your community—your board, staff, volunteers, donors, and beneficiaries—are excited and passionate about your ONE mission (as we hope they are). In that case, they will naturally talk about it in conversation, when they invite others to your events or decline invitations that conflict with them, or when they share your great news on their social media platforms. The ONE mission will flavor their discussions and color their world view. Your *audience* will be anyone within earshot of someone in your community or your people—like family, friends, acquaintances, book club members, yoga classmates, or local business owners. Your *audience* is those who will be reached by your earned and paid media, awareness campaigns, or fundraising efforts. Anyone within the personal, professional, and social circles of your community members are your *audience*.

Making Your Case

Developing your overarching *Case* is part and parcel of recognizing your current reality and creating a vision for where you want to go.

The *Case* for your nonprofit organization is the all-encompassing toolkit, the institutional history, and the current roadmap to get your people to the Promised Land. The *Case* exists so that if everyone on the board and staff of your organization got stranded on an island in the middle of an ocean tomorrow, a new team of do-gooders could walk in and pick up where you left off, without missing a beat.

If prepared well, your case is also the one-stop resource for planning, communications, and fundraising for your organization. Your *Case* standardizes the messaging that informs your grant proposals, media kits, annual communication plan, and individual fundraising campaign content. It informs your website, publications, and donor communications and is further developed by them. Your *Case* ensures that your historical and data-driven content is consistent across various channels and over time, especially if more than one person is responsible for donor cultivation.

Elevator Pitch

Consider your Case from the perspective of the elevator pitch cliché. Except imagine the elevator is heading up to the Observation Deck at the top of a skyscraper, like Chicago's John Hancock building (95 floors). As the doors close, you realize you're in the elevator with a group of billionaires who've taken the Giving Pledge.  Like Bill Gates and Warren Buffet, they've pledged to give away at least half of their wealth. The thing is, you aren't sure when they're getting off the elevator. What will you say when the billionaire next to you turns and extends a hand to introduce themselves?

Our automatic response is often name, rank, serial number. The name, position, place of employment trap: "I'm Jane Doe, executive director at ABC nonprofit?"

Ho-hum. Boring.

- *1-4 Floors – Problem & Big Vision*

What if, instead, you declare, "I'm creating a pipeline to professions." (*EnventU*)

Or "I give a voice to children in foster care." (*Court Appointed Special Advocates - CASA*). Or "I make sure girls in Uganda stay in school." (*The Mooncatcher Project*).

Like the first line of a well-written essay or novel, introducing your nonprofit to a stranger should be about hooking them and grabbing their attention, so they want to know more. The executive director of a food pantry might say, "I ensure that no child in Chicago goes to bed hungry." A faith-driven theatre company from Indiana (*all for One*) might say, "I make sure families have wholesome entertainment options in Ft. Wayne."

Notice you haven't mentioned anything about your job title, organization's name, nonprofit status, or the programs you offer. You've encapsulated the problem and vision.

Can't you just hear Oprah leaning in and saying, "Ooh, and how do you do that?"

- *5-10 Floors – Mission, tagline, solution highlights*

Once your billionaire is tuned-in and listening, and you've worked in your organization name and your title (executive director, board chair, volunteer), you can then share your solution and the value-added your organization brings to the equation.

Know your mission statement and taglines or mottos by heart. These shouldn't be complicated or long. If you struggle to remember these statements, work with leadership to rewrite them into easily memorized and understandable messages. You can even practice reciting them.

Focus on the core vision and values your solution embodies. Share program highlights and what you offer that differs from other organizations doing similar work.

When *EnventU*, an early-stage nonprofit in the DC area, shifted their language from "preparing youth to work in the event industry" to a mission of "creating a pipeline to professions," they cut to the heart of the issue. Without possibilities for a meaningful profession, many DC youth are likely to end up in prison. The simple phrase "pipeline to profession" captures the issues surrounding the school to prison pipeline, the prison industrial complex, and the lack of meaningful career opportunities with one quick phrase.

- *11-40 Floors – Impact & program details*

As the elevator climbs towards the 40th floor, highlight the impact of your solution with stories. Stories produce oxytocin and draw the listener into your passion. Your enthusiasm will be contagious. Anecdotal reports and results move the conversation from fanciful dreaming to meaningful change.

What impact has your work had on individuals and the broader community? When children eat well, how do they perform academically? When families spend time together, what happens to depression, delinquency, divorce, and domestic violence? When youth from under-resourced communities have access to resources, how does their genius explode? How many people have changed lives because of the work you do?

Latoya, the founder of *EnventU*, can talk about how the mission is changing the life trajectory for youth and disrupting the event industry as a whole. She can share their recently launched digital programming, custom interactive curriculum, and D.I.E. (Diversity, Inclusion, and Equity) initiatives.

Be proud of the accomplishments of your ONE mission and paint a picture for your listeners of how beautiful the Promised Land could be, what still needs to be done, and how far you are from it?

- *41-75 Floors – History, Key stakeholders/partners & hopes/dreams (strategic vision)*

Be ready with the organization's origin story, key milestones, and your personal catalyst for being involved. Know your key stakeholders and partners. Hearing the motivation of any prominent stakeholders offers credibility and legitimacy beyond anecdotes. If a billionaire is still listening on the 50th floor, you want to ensure them that others believe in you and support your efforts. Latoya can highlight significant industry partnerships with the school district, Boys & Girls Club, BizBash, and AVIXA.

If you're still struggling to find partners, knowing the current priorities (as outlined in your strategic plan) is crucial. Explain what you are looking for in a partner and what it would mean to your mission's trajectory. Where are you headed? Where do you want to go from where you are right now?

- *76-95 floors - Data, visionary budget*

As you near the top floors, you will want to discuss the next steps. Would the billionaire want more information? Do they need numbers? Demographic details? Studies and research to support your claims? Previous financials? The visionary budget? Might they want to hear more? Can you reach out? Should you follow up with someone?

You can see that the 95 floors elevator pitch is much more detailed than a few lines prepared for a quick two or three-story building. Your *Case* prepares you for every one of the 95 floors you travel with the billionaires. If your billionaire is still engaged when you get to the top floor, you will be ready to share links to the details of data, history, finances, and partnerships from the buttons of your phone. At the very least, you're prepared to do so the minute you return to your computer.

If you lay the skyscraper sideways, you have a briefcase or accordion file that contains every who, what, where, why, how, when, and what-for—your memory box, diary, and vision board rolled into one.

The Art of Persuasion: Pathos, Ethos, Logos, and Kairos

In developing your Case, the Art of Persuasion framework can help ensure that you have gathered all the elements you might need to answer questions from a potential granting foundation, donor, board member, employee, or volunteer in a way that appeals to everyone. Not everyone absorbs information or is moved to action in the same way. By having various perspectives prepared in advance, you can be ready to communicate in the way the prospective stakeholder can best hear it, without delay.

Four elements make up this framework:

- *Pathos*

Emotions: tell stories that paint a picture of urgency, need, problem. Be careful, do-gooder, to present a solvable puzzle. You can lead them to the brink of tears, but if they are full-on bawling and feeling overwhelmed, they won't have the inclination and power to act. Offer the hope that compels them to action. Let them know that the passion, compassion, anger, or enthusiasm they feel carries the

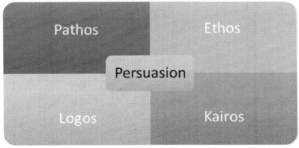

potential for change—if they act. Draw others into problem-solving action, not overwhelming despair.

- *Ethos*

Credibility: demonstrate that your organization is not only driven by a passion and vision but has the capacity and know-how to address issues effectively and efficiently. What talents and skills do you bring to the table to provide a solution in the scope you claim; prove you can (or already did) do what you say you will.

- *Logos*

Facts and Information: provide the information needed to understand the problem and how you're solving it; offer data; demonstrate impact. Prepare graphs, charts, infographics, and hard facts. While emotion tugs on heartstrings, if your data falls short, you'll struggle to retain foundation and donor support.

- *Kairos*

Opportunity and urgency: outline both the possibility and the urgency of this moment and the unique opportunity offered if they get involved. Why now? If the vision you present is too distant or removed from the listener's current reality or experience, they will be less likely to respond. If you don't provide a compelling reason for them to act right now or very soon, a more urgent and time-sensitive cause will draw their attention from your cause.

Contents of a Case

While every Case will differ, you would do well to include a wide range of elements to be ready at every opportunity to make your case in a way that a prospective donor needs to hear or see it. You likely have a great deal of this content on your website and computer or scattered across your desk. Now is the time to pull it all together!

- *Inspirational Origins*
  - Your WHY: cause, problem, puzzle, solution, impact
  - Why did this organization begin? What motivated the founder?
  - Why do you exist today?
  - What would happen if you ceased to exist? What would be the loss?
  - Whom do you serve?
  - How do you serve them differently from other organizations?

- *Mission Moment*
  - Mission statement
  - Vision statement
  - Core Values
  - Philosophy
  - Mottos and Taglines

- *Legal Legitimacy*
  - Articles of Incorporation
  - Bylaws
  - IRS Tax-Exempt Status documentation
  - Sales Tax Exemption letter
  - Annual list of board of directors
  - Board meeting agendas and minutes
  - Official annual report filings

- *Financials (3-5 year)*
  - P&L
  - Annual Budget
  - Program Budgets

- Audit results
- Donor Reports
- 990s
- Previous grants

- *Partnerships*
  - Major companies or organizations that support you
  - Major companies or organizations with whom you collaborate

- *History*
  - Major program milestones, solution pivots
  - Key leadership changes
  - Changes in location, buildings

- *Programs*
  - Program element outlines
  - Narratives that share perspectives
  - Ideal participant profile
  - Annual program results and impact
  - Desired program growth

- *Personnel*
  - Professional bio/resume for the founder, board members, leadership team, staff.
  - Narrative "WHY" for board members, key leadership, program directors, staff.

- *Testimonials*
    - Written or audio/visual recordings of WHY people are involved and the impact the organization has had on their lives and the cause.
        - Board members
        - Staff
        - Volunteers
        - Program participants or recipients of services

- *Strategic Goals*
    - High-level goals articulated in your strategic plan

- *Funding Priorities*
    - Wishlist for new programs on the horizon

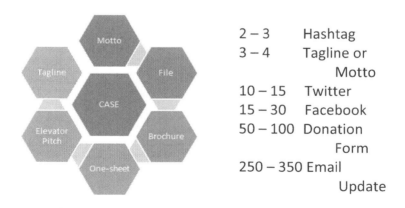

2 – 3	Hashtag
3 – 4	Tagline or Motto
10 – 15	Twitter
15 – 30	Facebook
50 – 100	Donation Form
250 – 350	Email Update

Boil Down Your Case

Your Case becomes the receptacle from which you cultivate a growth mindset throughout your organization. Once you've developed your entire Case, you'll also want to boil down your case into consumable segments. Begin creating a set of standard hashtags, taglines, and mottos to represent your "Why?" quickly and concisely. How do you capture the most inspiring and motivating elements of your history, programs and services, and impact? And how do you incorporate some of these elements into the communications you'll share on social media, in marketing and fundraising materials, and during personal donor cultivation meetings?

The Case is not a one-and-done final deliverable but is a living, ever-developing set of documents. As your organization grows, you write and gather more content. The newsletters and donor communications, the program descriptions, and the personnel bios get added to the Case and preserve your institutional history. Your Case becomes the "everything you need to know about your organization" in one place (preferably a folder stored in the cloud) for easy access.

With your Case in hand, the board, volunteers, and staff can become empowered as ambassadors, connectors, and influencers that will continue to bring your organization to the next level of excellence and get you all closer to the Promised Land.

The 7th Commandment

Thou shall NOT commit adultery.
Thou SHALL be loyal.

Right now, you are probably thinking: How does adultery even factor into the ten commandments for a nonprofit organization? And what does it have to do with communications?

Think about it, do-gooder. Isn't the pain and emotion surrounding adultery rooted in much more than physical betrayal? Is it not also about loyalty?

I better understood the concept of loyalty and the profound nature of what it means to be loyal when I learned how to speak and write Chinese. The Chinese character for loyalty is the symbol for *center* placed directly over the symbol for *heart*. Loyalty challenges us to reflect on what is most central to us. The 7th Commandment challenges every do-gooder—board member, employee, volunteer, and donor, to answer the question, "Where does your heart reside?"

Where is Your Heart?

Of course, I'm not suggesting that any nonprofit mission or cause should be the ONLY object of our loyalty. Faith, family, and friendships deserve our loyalty. And other nonprofit causes may deserve our loyalty.

Let's face it—when it comes to causes and missions, we have to pick. The world is far from perfect. Poverty, disease, injustice, and all the various *isms* that plague society can overwhelm someone with a good heart. And while we would love to save the whole world and solve every puzzle, we can't. We have to make choices for how we will allocate our time, talent, and treasure.

Building Loyalty

Significantly few people get involved as a board member, volunteer, staff, or donor with a nonprofit organization to do absolutely nothing. Something motivates them to get involved. The founder, executive director, and board members are responsible for ensuring that no stakeholder is indifferent or apathetic to your problem, solution, and impact. But exactly why these stakeholders engage could be different for everyone. Understanding their motivation is one of the first steps to building a long-lasting, meaningful relationship.

Motivation: The Catalyst

The board members of one early-stage nonprofit organization had been struggling for months to understand and commit to their role in fundraising. The founder was frustrated; the board members were disengaging. When we gathered for board training, I simply asked each member to share their WHY. How did they first hear about the organization? Why did they first get involved? Why were they still engaged and willing to serve on the board?

As each one listened to the other, visibly moved by the stories they heard. One had received services during a tough spot in her life. Another heard from a friend how his son had benefited from the organization. Still, another had been searching for an organization to offer her project management expertise where it would be most impactful, and the founder's passion inspired her.

When you discover what drew each person to your mission and why they got involved in the first place, you can better begin to understand their loyalty and how they will likely engage moving forward, and how to best nurture the relationship. In other words, you'll want to discover what was the catalyst that drew them to choose your mission as their own:

- *Lifetime Passion*

  Maybe you've always adored animals, you've danced and expressed yourself through movement your entire life, history has always intrigued you, or injustice infuriates you—and you never imagined doing anything but sharing your passion with the world.

- *Life Happened*

  Disease (Cancer, Multiple Sclerosis, Diabetes) or disaster (unemployment, homelessness) struck you or someone you love, and you want to make sure others never suffer in the same way.

- *Defining Moment*

  In an unexpected life-defining moment, you were knocked off your horse, blinded by the light, heard a calling, and took your first steps on a journey you never anticipated—and maybe even tried to resist.

- *Convenience or Need*

  You need a job, or you know volunteering or serving on a board is good for your resume. The stars aligned, and you could get behind the mission enough to make it work, but you could be equally supportive of another mission if it furthers your professional growth, pays your bills, or quiets your guilt.

Attitude: The Commitment Spectrum

Let me be clear, do-gooder. Just as it's possible for a parent to love more than one child, your board members, staff, volunteers, and donors can be passionate about more than one issue, mission, or organization. Caring about more than one problem or supporting more than one mission isn't adultery. Understanding why someone got involved with your mission is one step to an honest conversation about their loyalty to your mission and vision, but it isn't the only step.

To consider a stakeholder's loyalty, it is important to honestly and openly, without judgment, articulate each person's level of commitment from the perspective of time, talent, and treasure. You can't demand that everyone has martyrdom-like, full-blown enthusiasm for your mission. You can, at the very least, understand and respect where they might land on the following spectrum of commitment levels:

- *ALL-in (in it for the long haul)*

    These are the folks who live and breathe your organization. Their hands go up first. They give consistently. Their family and friends never stop hearing about your organization. They are loyal, and if you play your cards right, they always will be.

- *STAND-up (activist, advocate, protector)*

    Advocates and activists work on your behalf. They may not give at high levels, but they'll promote and defend your organization, even when it might be inconvenient. They'll use their power of influence and persuasion to bring others to your cause. They aren't afraid to let others know what you – and they – stand for, and you remain one of their top philanthropic or volunteer causes.

- *SHOUT-out (ambassador to share the story)*

Ambassadors care about what you care about. They wish the organization well, give when they can, and show up when possible. They care enough to promote your work when convenient but don't always put your mission first. While their primary loyalty and All-in commitment might be with another organization, they still value and support your vision.

- *DRIVE-thru (a resume builder, passing fancy, sense of guilt, it's a job)*

Like those motivated by convenience or personal need, a stakeholder who has joined your board, volunteers, or works in your organization with a drive-thru commitment level can be fiercely loyal during their stay and bring a great deal of time, talent, and treasure to the table. Think of the interim CEOs who turn a business around and leave it in better shape than when they arrived. Just because their relationship is temporary, and the motivation may be less than altruistic, the drive-thru stakeholder is a stakeholder, nonetheless. And who knows, they may become all-in lifers along the way.

Loyalty in Action

While attitude is undoubtedly essential, and everyone's motivations must be respected, mindset is meaningless without action. In your efforts to build loyalty, you can't ignore the importance of moving from attitude to action.

Community members set boundaries according to their level of commitment. Understanding and validating each person's relationship will reduce resentment and likely improve engagement of those whose engagement level has often been viewed as *less-than* instead of merely different.

When we begin to appreciate what each person brings to the table, they respond accordingly. To avoid dead weight and lack of action, encourage engagement even for those who cannot commit to being ALL-in. If someone commits to a few hours a month acting on behalf of the organization, celebrate that commitment.

Creating clear communication channels around which skills and talents someone wants to contribute is essential from the get-go. While your organization may be in desperate need of a legal mind, social media pro, or financial wizard, just because an individual's professional life demands these skills and talents, don't assume they want to offer these around the board room table or as a volunteer. Sometimes folks want to volunteer their time and talent in areas that are very different from their day job or careers. Others have hidden talents that you might never know about if you don't ask. Encourage conversations around hobbies, personal preferences, and how they see themselves having an impact.

As the core supporters for your organization, the board shares responsibility for ensuring your long-term fiscal viability. Not every board member needs to contribute the same monetary amount, but encouraging 100% board giving, at some level, goes a long way to building authenticity. When they engage in fundraising efforts among family, friends, and strangers, they aren't asking someone to do what they aren't willing to do. In this way, fundraising becomes a peer-to-peer interaction.

Some would argue that expecting board members to make a monetary contribution hinders efforts to build diversity or involve constituents in leadership. I would resist this generalization. If your board includes community members or constituents that would struggle to make a significant contribution, structure the invitation to give in a way that emphasizes participation instead of amount. On the one hand, it perpetuates the stereotype that people of color are low-income individuals lacking the capacity to give. On the other, it could imply that, for some reason, they lack the propensity to be philanthropic.

I believe with all my heart, do-gooder, that even the smallest gift makes a big difference. And inviting all board members to participate in collective generosity reinforces

---

Once a board member has made a personal contribution, their fundraising efforts among family, friends, and strangers becomes a peer-to-peer interaction. They are no longer asking someone to do what they aren't willing to do.

---

the culture of gratitude we discussed in the 5th Commandment and builds a more robust community.

Build Community

At this point, do-gooder, you might be asking, "But what does all this talk about loyalty have to do with creating a communications plan?"

While many organizations expect loyalty from their volunteers and donors, we sometimes forget that we, too, must be loyal. Once you understand how your community is loyal to your cause, your communications plan is the tool to demonstrate your loyalty to your community. As you develop your communications plan, don't forget to keep asking yourself: Where's my (our) heart? How am I (are we) showing loyalty to our community? How can I (we) be of service to our community?

Can One Size Really Fit All?

If you treat every person for whom you have an address, email, or phone number, in the same way, you aren't developing relationships. Of course, you can't put the same time and energy into building relationships with every event attendee, person in your database, or follower on social media. You can implement practices that foster authentic relationship building within the scope of your capacity.

I like to think of two parallel tracks for building community—personal encounters and the mass market, stadium-size approach. These two tracks correspond to what is commonly known as the 80/20 principle. From the Pareto Principle in economics, we've generally come to understand that 80% of revenue comes from 20% of donors, and 20% of revenue comes from the remaining 80% of the donor base. The principle is not set in stone, of course. Generally, though, if you look at your fundraising, you'll probably find that you have a small group of supporters who provide a good chunk of your resources. Some experts speak of a 90/10 and even a 95/5 breakdown in current philanthropy. Given the widening gap with wealth concentrated in the hands of the few, the trend towards a 95/5 principle is not surprising.

- *Personal Encounters*

Some folks might think that personal cultivation meetings don't belong in a communications plan. From my perspective, every opportunity to engage with your audience needs to be included in your communications plan—especially for small shops. You only have so many people involved in making it all happen. Looking at the entire picture and seeing where your time will be spent helps you right-size your expectations and build a realistic, sustainable plan.

Knowing the trend towards this 95/5 split, you'll want to ensure that you are building strong relationships with the small group of your highest-end donors because they are clearly invested in the cause. They aren't better than you or smaller gift donors. They don't deserve more respect. But you'd struggle to sustain the impact you have without their support, so getting to know them better and letting them know the impact they're having will keep them engaged in bringing the vision to reality. Ensuring that you're creating opportunities to engage in personal one-on-one or small group conversations and dialogue with these individuals to better understand their vision needs to be identified in your overall communications plan.

Many small organizations are so busy managing day-to-day operations that they don't allocate resources to the cultivation and stewardship of high-end donors. Some think they're too small to have a major gifts program; others are hesitant or feel unprepared to conduct personal cultivation meetings with donors. Remember do-gooder, donors who give (or have the capacity and propensity to give) at high levels care about what you care about just like you do. They want to make a difference, and they chose to do that by giving money to your mission.

Don't forget, do-gooder, we have a responsibility to confront systemic racism and inequities. Our cultivation and stewardship of these high-gift donors do not excuse us from our obligation. We can't let the possibility of losing a major donor's support stop us from challenging the very structures that create the existing and ever-widening wealth and equality gap.

As we build a relationship with these donors who can make high-level donations, we position ourselves to have what may be more challenging conversations. If they are unaware, we can provide insight into the root causes of the problem we may be addressing and invite them to make transformational gifts. Indeed, our engagement with individuals with high capacity could also lead to connections and relationships with those who have more power. Money can mean power—the power to make change possible.

- *Mass Market*

On the flip side of personal engagement with the top 10-20% of your donor base is the mass market approach to community engagement. As I said, small gift donors don't deserve less respect or loyalty than major donors. Perhaps my mother's devotion to filling her weekly church envelope with $2 from her meager paycheck each Sunday has influenced my perspective. Or maybe it's the widow's mite parable, where Jesus praised the pittance offered by a poor woman over that given from others' abundance. Since you can't meet personally with everyone, you'll need to decide how you will engage the remainder of your audience?

When most people think of a communications plan, they're thinking of written communications. Your plan doesn't need to be limited to the written word. Holding fundraising events is one of the most common ways for an organization to communicate with a broad audience. We'll discuss events a bit more in the fundraising section, but for now, think about the different opportunities you might have for engaging with donors in groups (even if pandemic safety protocols restrict you in 2020-2021).

Beyond events, you'll also want to include paid and earned media options. How often, and in what situations, will you pay for advertising? Can you gain media coverage by offering expertise to the local media outlets, business chambers, or professional associations? Will you send out press releases for specific activities or events? Will you participate in community events (when they are available)?

Again, you may not immediately think of these types of activities as part of your communications plan. But if you're creating conversations with the community, people, and audience that share your vision and values, include these activities in your plan.

- *Personalized*

On my birthday this year, I received many emails wishing me well. These weren't from friends but from businesses like the bank that holds my car loan, Starbucks, and my dentist. They each include the line, "Happy Birthday, Janet!" These businesses have technology that automates personalized messages. No human being had to be involved in creating it beyond entering my name into the database once. They didn't *mean* much to me—although I appreciated the free beverage from Starbucks. At the very least, they didn't feel entirely impersonal and generic.

In the age of the digital merge, sending "Dear Friend" communications feels lazy. Even if you don't know everything about me, at the very least, attempt to personalize communications. Demonstrate that you recognize I am one person among many, not an unidentifiable collective. Personalization should be the bare minimum. Even if you don't have a donor management platform, if you use an email service like MailChimp or Constant Contact, you should be able to manage a first name merge.

That said, if you can't merge the name of a person into your email or direct mail communications, I read recently where Dr. Kiki Koutmeridou suggested using a "Dear *Org Name* Supporter" salutation rather than "Dear Friend." Using the supporter language will make them tune in to their role as a supporter and trigger support, whereas calling them a friend might feel *sales-y* and unnatural (https://sofii.org/article/ask-a-behavioural-scientist-part-three).

- *Personal*

To make personalization personal, a person needs to act. Personal interaction happens when a person is involved in initiating communication with another person. A phone call, a handwritten signature or envelope, a note in the corner, a sticky note with a message specific to the reader. What capacity do you have to un-automate your relationship building?

If you have an extensive database, you may not be able to make every communication personal. But with a little forethought, you can identify opportunities to make communications personal for different segments of your donor base at various times throughout the year.

Identify which criteria you'll use to decide who receives personal communications—institute a major gifts program for high-level donors who might, perhaps, receive personal communications most often. Create a cycle for handwritten notes to all recurring, monthly donors throughout the year. Enlist the board, staff, volunteers, and even beneficiaries in the process of personal communications when appropriate and possible.

The more personal the touch, the more connected and engaged the audience will feel. Even when you're using a mass marketing approach to communicating, you have plenty of tools at your fingertips to engage your community on a very personal level, at least some of the time.

Donor-Centric Communications

A healthy communication plan integrated with fundraising goals and objectives will incorporate a cyclical approach of sharing success and presenting a need to ensure donors are thanked and informed of mission impact as often, if not more than, you ask them for money.

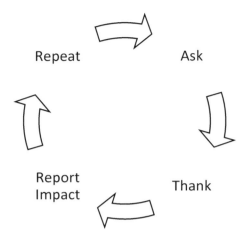

Repeat   Ask

Report Impact   Thank

- *Cultivate Supporters*

The supporter cultivation cycle can be summed up with four simple words: *ask, thank, report, repeat.* Although the donor relationship typically doesn't begin with the ask, once someone donates to your organization, you'll want to ensure that they move into this cyclic communication approach so that not every communication becomes an ask.

- **Ask** – share an unfinished story of need and have a clear call to action
- **Thank** – show appreciation and tell them what their donation is doing
- **Report Impact** – share a success story, let them know what they helped accomplish
- **Repeat** – repeat the cycle

The more you communicate gratitude and report impact, the more. often you can repeat the cycle and ask for more support. Too many nonprofits are stuck on the idea of sending a newsletter. They gather various stories and statistics to share as they did with a two- or four-page print document that would traditionally be mailed monthly or quarterly to keep the community informed.

I encourage my clients who are using email to communicate at least monthly. Ideally, if you have plenty going on, you can touch base weekly or twice a month. E-communications can be more current and much shorter. You could link to an article or a quick video or offer a highlight or spotlight on a program. Rather than thinking of a formal newsletter, develop a conversational tone, and share anecdotes. While you shouldn't merely communicate for the heck of it, the fact is that if you're trying to get to the Promised Land, you have to let people know.

- *Tell a Compelling Story*

Your language arts teacher in grade school was correct in teaching you, "Show; don't tell." Don't tell your donors that kids attend camp or adults get jobs. Instead, through your stories, show confident kids forging friendships or adults beaming with pride as they provide for their children. When the donor empathizes with the individual's fears, desires, and hopes in the story they read, your WHYs become one.

Like a great piece of literature, your storytelling will transform a personal incident or circumstance into a universal experience. The donor wants to find their story inside yours.

Introducing an individual in need with whom a prospective donor can relate, you draw them into the universal emotion of a struggling protagonist and allow them to accompany that individual, not your organization, on their journey.

- *Tug at the Heart*

Don't worry, do-gooder, I'm not talking about getting mushy or falling into trauma or poverty porn. Instead of the sad, puppy-dog eyes commercials with miserable music playing in the background, think Subaru. What does Subaru sell?

If you answered, "Love," you know what I'm talking about. "Love: It's what makes a Subaru a Subaru." Coldwell Banker's COVID-19 commercials aren't selling houses; they're selling "Home." Ford sells "Tough." Kay Jewelers sells "kisses" because "every kiss begins with K." The most recent FedEx commercial I saw said, "Miracles. It's what we deliver by delivering." If FedEx can deliver miracles, I think we can too.

When you write your communications, tap into the core emotion that will connect to your reader or listener. What do your services REALLY offer to your beneficiaries and your donors? What are their deepest desires? What do they care about? Will donating to your organization help them accomplish that?

- *Mind Your Words*

In your donor communications, pay attention to the language you use. Avoid phrases like "partner with us," "help us to," and "so that we can." Words and sentence patterns that subtly or not so subtly imply that the organization is the hero do not really honor the donor's role. In fact, for many nonprofits, without donors, there is no mission. In these cases, donors make the mission happen, and the vision a reality. Make sure they know how important they are.

Use active verb + noun phrases in your writing. Speak to the WHY or WHAT and for WHOM: educate a child, empower a girl, teach a future scientist, find a forever home for a dog, heal a sick child, uplift a community through music or theater. Explain in vivid, tangible terms how a gift or investment will impact another person or animal. Don't relegate the donor to *helper* or *assistant* status. Let the hero shine.

Remember, you want to write to one person. Only one person is reading the letter. Phrases like "donors like you" and "you and other generous donors" make the reader feel like one in a crowd. Is your donor one *of* a million heroes or the one *in* a million who is a hero because they care? If you have so many wonderful donors, you probably don't need me.

- *Make the donor the hero!*

One way to create the one in a million feeling for the donor is to let their inner hero shine. Heroes act selflessly, making a difference when it isn't required of them. Heroes change lives. Heroes save lives. If you are thanking a donor for a gift, focus on the impact the donor made. Share the happy ending. The donor's generosity has changed a life in some way, shape, or form—be sure they know it.

Are you asking for money? Ensure that every potential donor knows they can be a hero by giving a gift, no matter how small. Write an unfinished story where their action impacts the ending. If they donate, you all move closer to the vision you share.

Remember, do-gooder, making one donor the hero doesn't lessen any other donor, volunteer, or beneficiary's hero-ness. Every person has their own journey, their own moment to shine.

Communicate your Message

Communicating the problem you are solving with urgency and compunction, juxtaposing with the impact your work has had on getting to the Promised Land, is a delicate art. Too much emphasis on the critical, urgent problem can lead to your audience feeling overwhelmed and defeated. A dooms-dayer inspires no one. On the flip side, too much bragging about the success you've had could send the message that everything is hunky-dory, and you don't need help.

Create Collateral Materials

For many years in the classroom, I created lesson plans based on Howard Gardner's *Multiple Intelligences* theory. While different approaches have replaced the emphasis on multiple intelligences, individuals have preferences for how they consume and process information, simple as that. Some folks need visuals; others prefer to hear explanations. Others don't fully process information until they've put it into their own words or analyzed the evidence themselves.

As a nonprofit leader, you want to be ready for these various types of "learners" by preparing a variety of resources and utilizing several channels of communication. Then those who care about what you care about get the information and engagement they need.

And, do-gooder, don't think you need to reinvent the content each time you communicate. Reuse, recycle and revamp content to fit into different formats to share in specific circumstances. And if you aren't the creative type or don't have the capacity, search for someone to help.

Look for interns, volunteers, or independent contractors; checkout free resources that make developing creative materials easy. At the time of this writing, Canva (canva.com) seems to be a popular service for many organizations. If you join a few social media groups for nonprofit marketing and communications, you can gather all sorts of great ideas. Don't be afraid to ask what others do. You aren't alone on this journey.

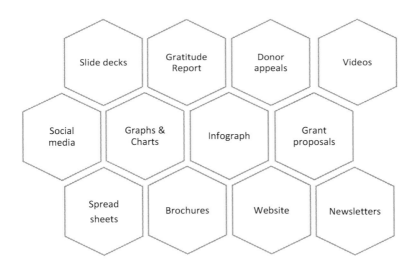

Examples of Collateral Materials

Decide on Communication Channels

When creating your communication plan, you want to consider how you're going to reach your community, people, and audience. Don't try to do everything everyone else does – if it doesn't fit your community. Think about where your people reside? How do they communicate with one another? Where do they like to receive their information? How can you break through the noise, so they hear you?

In creating your communication plan, you'll need to decide which tools you'll use to engage. You may rely heavily on print communications because you have physical addresses for your stakeholders? Or you have a robust E-mail list, so that is the best tool for you? Do you have a social media presence? Which platform works for your community, people, and audience? Where do they live in cyberspace? What access do you have for making format and content changes to your website?

I highly recommend that you take the time to explore your different options for multi-channel communications. No one size fits all when it comes to direct mail, email, and social media—not to mention video, phone, and text messaging. The more channels you have to reach your audience, the more effective your communications will be. But don't rush into making these decisions and hopping on every bandwagon without considering how you will measure effectiveness and productivity with each channel you might use. And whatever you do, do-gooder, don't forget that you are trying to create conversation and dialogue, not merely shout to the wind about how great your organization is.

Assign Responsibility

One part of developing your communications plan is deciding who'll be in the driver's seat. Do you have one person (paid or volunteer) who is the *Chief Everything Officer* responsible for driving programs, communications, and fundraising? Do you have a *Writer Extraordinaire* who handles all communications and simply needs to know what stories to tell and when? Do you have a *Social Media Savvy* staff or stakeholder who loves nothing more than to make your organization go viral? Once you've identified how many drivers you have and who's in the driver's seat for each engagement opportunity, assess your capacity to communicate throughout the year.

Establish Your Calendar

Once you've decided who will and how to share your case, you'll need to determine when. What is your capacity to engage with those who care about what you care about? Do you have the time to find others to join you? How often can/should you post to social media? Send emails? Send snail mail? Meet with donors? You get the idea, I'm sure.

- *Consistency*

Aim for quality (not perfection) and consistency over frequency.

Like so many other do-gooders in the early stages of trying to build a dream, Jill had a full-time job to keep it all going. Together, we developed a strong vision, articulated clear messaging, and discussed her ideal communications plan for personal donor stewardship and the mass market approach to donor cultivation. She struggled to be consistent—and she grew frustrated.

Her communications were more sporadic than she'd hoped, so much so that she wanted to pass up a local, regional giving day because she felt disloyal to her donors. As the day rolled around, she pulled together and sent out an email, which she was certain no one would read. To her surprise, not only did many donors open her email, two major donors called her directly, offering impactful gifts that arrived at a critical time for her program calendar.

Because we'd spent time developing important, impactful messaging for this organization, the founder could quickly and effectively take advantage of an opportunity.

Consistency keeps you front of mind, instills trust, and creates an ongoing conversation between you and your audience. Consistency also creates more opportunity to engage in meaningful dialogue, especially on social media.

You may not always meet every deadline or hit every target in your communication plan. Having a clear message and scheduling touchpoints on your calendar will get you much further than simply communicating when the whim hits you or you "fit it in."

If you try to cram too much into your calendar, you might find yourself skipping too often. Then begins the cycle of self-blame, disappointment, and discouragement, ultimately scrapping your plan altogether. Make a note of what works and what doesn't so when you sit down next year, you'll be able to adjust accordingly. Let your calendar work for you, not become a burden.

Creating a Communications Plan

As we've said before, folks don't get excited about backing a budget; they embrace a vision! But they can't say "yes" to a vision and mission they don't understand. Your communication plan details the methods, message, and timeline for making your vision public and creating a relationship with those who care about what you care about.

The first step in creating a communications plan is to pull together the various documents and files that will become your Case. Once your Case is in order, you'll need to determine how you will engage.

Step 1. Decide <u>With Whom</u>

Decide who will be receiving your communications. Consider different identifiers to create segments. You may not send different communications to each group, but you could tweak a standard message with a few opening phrases or differing ask amounts without too much time or difficulty. Or you can decide to create a unique narrative for each group but send them at different times throughout the year.

Consider different criteria that would influence how a supporter might respond to a message. What message might resonate most? How would this particular group want to hear from you? What attitude or tone would they appreciate? What would trigger a response? Instead of treating your community, people, and audience as one monolithic group, consider the world and your organization from their perspective and their relationship to you.

Different subgroups (or segments) might hear you differently and need different communication styles. Possible segments you might consider could include:

a. Giving History
    i.   Donor – Non-donor – Lapsed Donor
    ii.   Major donor – Mid-level donor – Smaller donor
    iii.   Consistent donors: monthly recurring or annual
b. Affiliation
    i.   Which program inspires their giving?
    ii.   Did they or a loved one participate in a program?
    iii.   Do they always respond to the same topic?
    iv.   Are they a current or former volunteer?
c. Generation
    i.   Greatest and Silent
    ii.   Boomers and Gen X
    iii.   Millennials and Gen Y and Z
d. Contact information
    i.   Physical address and/or landline #
    ii.   Email and/or mobile phone
    iii.   Social media follower only

Don't be afraid to think outside the box. Can you think of other criteria that would impact how you will communicate with your community, your people, and your audience?

Step 2. Determine Where and How

Knowing exactly where and how to reach your audience can be challenging. You likely have contact information for those in your community, so you'll simply need to observe their engagement behavior to decide the best means to reach them. You could also conduct a survey to ask about their preferences.

Beyond your current community, you'll want to continue to grow. Where will you meet your supporters? Are they likely to be online or off? Would they be on social media, and if so, which platform? Do they watch local community television or listen to public radio? Would they pick up the local paper? Do they prefer email or text messaging? Do they love getting something in the mail?

Answering some of these questions will get you thinking about the various avenues available to connect with both current and potentially new supporters of your cause. And if you aren't sure where your people are, you may need to try something new.

Ultimately, you'll need to break through the background noise of life with a message that resonates. But if you haven't explored where your audience might be and what tools and tactics you'll use to reach them, your communications may be like the proverbial tree falling in the forest—will anybody hear it?

Step 3. Calendar When (and How Often)

Many nonprofits worry about communicating too often, but most nonprofits don't communicate enough. Taking these eight steps to create your calendar will help you find the balance between not enough and too much, focusing on right-sized consistency.

1. Begin with an annual calendar – either standard or fiscal year.
2. Insert any fundraising or program events that will demand your time and attention or require communications.

169

3. *Don't forget vacation time and essential family functions!* If you are busy with life, you'll have less time and energy to crank out organizational communications.

4. Work backward from the program date or event to block marketing and other functions that will consume your time.

5. Make a note of board and committee meetings, staff retreats, and other obligations that may not involve external communications but will still demand your time and attention.

6. Determine how much time you'll devote to communicating in person. In-person communication could include networking events, small group meetings with stakeholders, onsite visits or open houses, and individual donor cultivation meetings. In a small shop, the same person might handle all of these channels, so you can't forget to allocate enough time.

7. Carve out November and December for year-end communications that will likely focus on a fundraising appeal. Try not to shove too many other communication pieces into this period. You want to create an ongoing narrative with a range of engagement and emotion that carries the supporter through the season.

8. Decide when you'll share impact reports, success stories, good news, and program updates. Remember, do-gooder, you need something to say. The more you have going on, the more often you can share. Quarterly, monthly, bi-weekly, or weekly? Which day of the week and what time of day?

Don't let the perfect get in the way of the point—engagement.

Platform	January	February	March	etc.		Type of Communications	Strategic Goal	Cultivation Goal
	New Year's Resolutions National Pizza Week Martin Luther King, Jr. Day	Black History Month American Heart Health Groundhog Day Super Bowl Sunday Chinese New Year	International Women's Day St. Patrick's Day World Water Day			*Create drop-down menus to choose from*		
Donor Prospect Engagement						In Person meeting	Goal 1. Objective 1.	Ask
Major donor						Zoom meeting	Goal 1. Objective 2.	Thank
Donor						Video Message	Goal 1. Objective 3.	Report impact
Recurring donor						Text Message	Goal 2. Objective 1.	etc.
New donor						Telephone		
Lapsed donor						Private email		
Donor						Email Blast		
Recurring donor						Handwritten Note		
Lapsed donor						Personalized Letter		
Recurring donor						Form letter		
Donor						Virtual event		
Lapsed donor						In person event		
Previous corporate sponsor								
New corporate sponsor								
Previous corporate partner								
New corporate partner								
General Communications								
Website Updates								
Social Media Posts (# / week)								
Announcements								
Impact Updates								
Surveys/Polls								
Open-ended engagement questions								
Fundraising Link								
Impact on time/capacity								
Special Events (in person or virtual)								
Awareness Raising								
One off niche money raising								
Community building fundraiser								
Budget critical annual fundraiser								
Grants								
LOI								
Full applications								
Reporting								
Board Meeting								

Sample Communications

Step 4. Articulate *What*

Your strategic plan and your Case contain a wealth of content to pull from for your messaging. Your task in creating your communications plan is to decide what content to share, when, with whom. At this point in your planning, decide (at least at a high level) each communication topic. Your program calendar, the time of year, the audience, and possibly even current events will influence your messaging.

How are you incorporating the vision put forth in your strategic plan in your communications? Which strategic goal/objective are you sharing, addressing, furthering with this communication? Know which programs might offer a great story to tell—before or after.

Check out the lists of national holidays and awareness months/weeks/days related to your cause. How might you join a movement rather than merely comment by communicating during this time? By planning, you can gather the information you'll need because you'll see what's coming down the road. At the same time, you'll want to be agile enough to change your messaging if anything significant happens.

Step 5. Identify Why Now

Remember Kairos from the Art of Persuasion from the 6th Commandment? When you calendar your communications and articulate your theme or topic, don't forget to identify what makes this communication timely. Why is it, or should it be, important to the audience? How should they respond? What do you want them to do? What is the call to action? Every direct communication with your supporters needs to include a call to action. Your *why now* creates that call to action.

Step 6. Assign Responsibility

Who will handle each communication? Do you have different individuals responsible for separate tasks? Do you have a fundraiser who needs to coordinate with a social media manager? Will board members participate? If so, what lead time do they need to accomplish their tasks? When you review your entire plan, including everyone involved in a specific communication, you'll be able to honor each person's boundaries, respect their time and talent, and ensure that no person carries too much of the load.

Step 7. Engage Consistently

Review your entire plan to ensure that it is doable? You want to be consistent, especially with your current community. Do what you're already doing exceptionally well. Then, introduce new opportunities for engagement. Don't bite off more than you can chew. If any month or week looks too overwhelming, thin it out. If one channel is easier to manage and has the potential for furthering your reach, allocate more energy to it. If you're trying new approaches, make sure they aren't your only touchpoints during the assigned timeframe.

The more specific your plan, the better. Otherwise, you just have an idea, not a plan. But **please remember** that your communications plan, calendar, channel, and message don't have to be perfect. Your communication plan articulates the ideal, but even if you can't always live up to the ideal, don't stop engaging.

Promised Land

Part IV: Fundraising: Commandments 8 – 10

"Martin Luther King didn't get up 50 years ago and say: I have a budget and a plan!"

Ian Clayton

Having gone from growing up on welfare to living with a vow of poverty for 13 years, you could say my relationship with money has been awkward.

For years, I swore I could never be in sales because I didn't like money. And since fundraising was all about asking people for money, I wouldn't want to do that either. I didn't realize that while the goal of fundraising is to get money, the *ask* is only a small part of a fundraiser's job. Fundraising isn't just about asking for money.

Notice, I didn't say fundraising has *nothing* to do with money or that a fundraiser doesn't have to ask for money. Believe me, you do.

But fundraising is NOT *all about asking* for money. The truth is, fundraising has everything to do with inspiring action through educating and raising awareness about issues or promoting a passion, cultivating relationships with those who care and providing an opportunity for donors to experience the joy of giving.

Fundraising is not really ABOUT money. Fundraising is about inspiring and encouraging impact. Fundraising is connecting people who care about the same cause. Fundraising is about gathering those who want to get to the same Promised Land to participate in a collective effort.

That said, making an "ASK" is an integral part of fundraising.

Commandments 8-10 focus on the steps you can take to increase fundraising effectiveness once you've declared your vision (your Promised Land) and priorities (strategic plan) and encouraged others to join you (communications plan).

The 8th Commandment

Thou shall NOT steal.
Thou SHALL stop begging.

Ok, do-gooder, you're probably thinking, "Of course, I won't steal anything. Don't be silly."

Except for the occasional news headline, "local nonprofit director arrested for embezzlement," we like to assume outright stealing is not a massive issue at most nonprofits. But it certainly isn't unheard of. During this book's writing alone, several high-profile cases of questionable management hit mainstream media (NRA, We Build the Wall, WE Charity), demonstrating that sometimes do-gooders aren't as good as they appear.

Before getting into the details of what it means not to steal and to stop begging, let's pause for another moment to think about the act of giving.

Joy Someone

People give for a wide variety of reasons—often more than one reason at any given point in time. The fact that we remind donors their gift "is tax-deductible to the extent of the law" implies that some people give to charity for non-altruistic reasons, at least in part. By our very nature, humans tend to make choices based on what we perceive to be the better of two options, even if others disagree or a choice seems objectively bad. The person choosing finds some good in it even if the world disagrees. We may not consciously realize it, but we give because not giving feels like the less good option. In other words, giving makes us feel good. Neurologically, when we do something to help someone else, our brain releases the same "happy hormone" (i.e., dopamine) as when we receive a gift. Giving gives us joy. Literally.

When you ask someone to donate to your cause, you are spreading, inviting, encouraging joy.

So, go ahead, do-gooder—joy someone.

Keep Clean Records

Ideally, your organization has an accounting system and a separate electronic donor management system to track all in-kind and monetary donations. But, as we've already pointed out, we don't live in an ideal world. These systems can be costly. So, in the meantime, do-gooder, do good. Whether in an old fashion notebook or journal or a computer document, track every single transaction that occurs in support of your organization. You cannot have too many records with too much detail. Like your Case is your institutional messaging history, you want to create Records for your institution's transactional history.

Decide early on—or right now, how you will record financial transactions, in-kind donations, volunteer hours. Often, organizations don't establish standard operating procedures for various transactions, ending with messy, inaccurate data. Know how you record anything of value and codify it with policy and procedure manuals, so it doesn't change with each personnel change. Your methods don't need to be fancy or expensive; they just need to be consistent and accurate.

Checks and Balances

Whether we focus on community-centric fundraising that centers community members as the heroes of their own story or invest in donor-centric fundraising that centers the donor as the hero, we can't ignore the fact that monetary donations make a difference.

At the very least, we're obligated to protect the community's assets and put them to the best use possible. So, let's make sure we're neither stealing nor begging in the process.

Unfortunately, you can't simply assume no one will steal.

Derrick, the performing arts teacher at a small private high school, was confused by the lower ticket sale revenue each Friday night compared to Saturday and Sunday performances, despite the similar crowd sizes. The numbers didn't seem to reflect crowd size accurately. One weekend, his regular volunteers couldn't "handle the door" and, suddenly, that Friday had higher ticket sales than any night on the previous two years of Friday night sales. After a bit of investigating, Derrick discovered his regular Friday box office volunteers (upstanding parents of three children in the school) had been skimming sales. He quietly and politely informed them he'd no longer need their services, but few people knew why. Like many do to avoid a scene, he simply resolved the problem quietly, and everyone moved on.

No one wants to be suspicious of other do-gooders. And, hopefully, your volunteers and employees are trustworthy and upright citizens. But as I always say, "Leadership's responsibility is to protect the organization from any one individual."

Creating policies and procedures that provide a system of checks and balances in financial management ensures that literal stealing won't happen within your organization.

In this age of technological efficiency, clients ask about having their donor management system speak directly to their accounting system. We want everything done with the click of a button. I get the attraction to simplify steps and reduce redundancy, but I recommend caution. In small, all-volunteer, or skeleton staff organizations, it might be tough to divide the work, but we have to create a process of checks and balances. The person responsible for receiving and logging donations should not be responsible for posting accounts receivable or preparing bank deposits or signing all the checks. Fundraising and financial tracking should be separated and managed by different individuals to allow for monthly reconciliation of accounting and donor reports.

Mismanagement of Funds

Tanya, the new executive director of an established organization with an $8 million budget, was informed the organization had paid off all their debt during the hiring process. About six weeks into her tenure, the bookkeeper told her that a stack of unpaid bills sat in a drawer in the finance office and that vendors refused to deliver products without upfront payment. The unpaid bills totaled more than $400,000.

With a bit more probing, Tanya soon deduced that the organization was facing a $1,000,000 deficit on the year between unpaid bills and uncollected fees for service.

No one had physically stolen a penny, but the house certainly wasn't in order.

Tanya, not wanting to throw good money after bad, believed she couldn't ask donors for another penny until she straightened out the mess.

Fortunately, a key stakeholder's friend was a forensic auditor between jobs who agreed to work with her, pro-bono, to review the situation. In addition to redirecting funds to the administration's pet projects, they had double-paid bills, payments to vendor accounts they no longer did business with, insurance payments for deceased employees, mistakes in accounting—the list went on.

Financial Reporting

How did the mismanagement and waste Tanya discovered happen in the first place? The finance director presented a monthly report showing revenue and expense and variance against the current and previous years' budgets. The finance committee had been reviewing the numbers and fretting over concerns about cash flow. Still, no one questioned the report's validity until a new board member asked for something he knew the accounting software could generate.

Only then did Tanya and the board discover that the finance director had been using the robust and expensive accounting software only to print checks. They hadn't performed software updates in years, despite updates being offered in the contract agreement. He didn't follow accounting best practices, and he constructed the monthly reports manually, using a calculator and spreadsheets. With a few phone calls and two hours of training, the system was updated and ready to go. Tanya instituted checks and balances to protect the organization from future mismanagement concerns.

Tanya didn't approach donors during these six months. She identified the mismanaged accounts payable and receivable, cut expenses wherever possible, and implemented policy and procedures to ensure accurate revenue from service fees. The organization took a loan on a credit line to get through the year and presented a budget with a $2 million reduction in expenses without cutting any programs. She improved profitability without sacrificing service.

When Tanya could honestly and authentically ensure that she would put donors' money to good use, she shared her vision for the future and asked stakeholders to help make it happen.

By the anniversary of her hire date, she had repaid half the loan and had money in the bank to repay the remainder of that deficit before year-end. The fact that Tanya cut one-quarter of the budget without negatively impacting programming caught the attention of major donors who'd previously stopped supporting the organization. They appreciated that Tanya was willing to manage the business, reduce the waste, and put their money towards a vision they all believed possible. Donors returned.

Overhead: Madness, Myth or Magic

We can't ignore the critical question of nonprofit overhead when discussing the commandment not to steal. The frequency of articles and opinion pieces that rail against nonprofit CEO salary and what it costs for an organization to raise a dollar compels the conversation.

If you've ever completed a grant application or dug into a discussion about nonprofit budgets, you've heard concern about how much an organization should spend on "overhead." Some watchdog groups and websites rate organizations based on these percentages irrespective of the good they do.

Given our earlier discussion about profitability, you know I'm a cheerleader for cost-effectiveness. We should prepare for profitability but the preoccupation with "overhead" baffles me. Who decided that the money that keeps the lights on for your programs is less important than the funds that go directly to programs? And doesn't time spent fundraising also support programs? Without the money to pay operational expenses, you have no means to deliver the mission.

Somewhere along the way, people began equating nonprofit overhead with "waste"—but is it? The logic goes, if we don't pay employees too much and we don't spend too much on the tools we need to bring our services to market, we are better, nobler, and more worthy of support.

When we purchase a product, do we ask what percent of the cost is paying for overhead? Or do we look at the benefits and value-added of the product and consider the purpose it serves for the price we pay? Aren't most folks willing to pay more for a meal that tastes great and provides exceptional service than for one that doesn't?

That said, the discrepancy between the haves and have-nots in this country, particularly in recent years, is the fodder for anger, angst, and political advocacy for many. Couple this with the exorbitant for-profit CEO salaries, not to mention the golden parachutes they receive even as they're run from their companies in shame after a scandal. Who wants to see one individual make six figures while others don't make a living wage? I've personally thought, more than once, "This can't be right! That's stealing!"

When the top 1% holds more wealth than the bottom 99%, those in the 99% can't help but feel like something is desperately wrong. These realities have brought renewed attention to the question of what constitutes appropriate compensation and non-program spending at nonprofits.

At this point, do-gooder, you're probably thinking, "I barely make five figures, much less 6 or 7," and "What does this gotta do with stealing anyway?"

I can hear you screaming, "Most nonprofits don't pay enough!"

I know. Stick with me.

Many nonprofit professionals are underpaid relative to their education, skillset, and responsibility compared to their for-profit counterparts, which drives many to leave the nonprofit sector. I've heard board members insist that the paid employees "don't do this for the money" and "no one should be paid too much" as an excuse for offering ridiculously low salaries.

Just like "being busy" to the point of exhaustion is not noble, neither is not paying your employees a decent wage. We should offer a competitive salary that screams, "Your skills, your genius, and your dedication will get us to the Promised Land. We value what you bring to the table." If we paid those responsible for mission delivery what they deserve, perhaps many of the ills that plague our efforts would vanish.

More often, the opposite is true. We stretch too thin, trying to do more with too little (remember our discussion on mission creep) that we forget donors support us so that we can do better. As the old saying goes, we try to be penny-wise but end up being pound foolish.

Many nonprofits put up with old computers, inadequate facilities, and an under-qualified workforce to save money. Allowing employees to work in less than desirable conditions or not providing the proper tools to get the job done effectively also perpetuates a scarcity mindset. Operating your programs and services with outdated and inefficient equipment does not serve the mission. When we aren't delivering the best service or product possible because we are afraid to waste "too much," we are guilty of stealing from both the donor and the beneficiaries we serve.

Be Efficient and Effective

As the newly hired vice president of advancement for a small health clinic, Matthew led a nine-person development department, including communications and marketing and all aspects of fundraising and donor relations. Over the previous several years, the department had become bloated. Rather than deal with the ineffectiveness or inefficiency of a staff person, equipment, or procedures, they hired additional staff to make up for the deficiencies. The department was oversized relative to the program staff and participants, not to mention their fundraising outcomes. Comparing the salary cost alone to the department's revenue, Matthew realized the department was costing the organization money.

After just a few conversations with key stakeholders, Matthew learned that major donors with business savvy had been holding back their giving for years because they had questioned the organizational infrastructure. By rightsizing the department and hiring four competent professionals to replace the nine, Matthew drastically reduced expenses but, more importantly, substantially increased gross and net fundraising revenue.

Don't get me wrong. I'm not saying all development and fundraising offices are ineffective or that you should not pay fundraising professionals a competitive wage. I'm also not asserting that money is the only thing that matters or that every aspect, task, or tactic of the fundraising department needs to have a specific monetary return on investment. Fundraising is a long game with the results sometimes not seen for years, but that doesn't excuse poor management or low productivity.

Right-size

Whether you operate with too few staff or a few too many, learning to right-size your organization is a critical step to keeping the commandment not to steal. Paying one highly qualified individual and giving them the resources and an appropriate salary to do the job, is better than paying less competent people a lower wage for doing substandard work.

Yes, yes. I know. In an ideal world! Who has the money!

Funding can be an issue, often because we lack the vision to see beyond our current capacity. We get sucked into a scarcity mentality, and we lack the conviction that basic efficiency is critical. Spending money upfront can save time and money in the long run—time and money better spent on increasing your impact.

Once you clearly articulate how you can efficiently and effectively provide a solution to the problem, you can tell your story and approach fundraising with the authenticity that will catch donors' attention. You will then be able to hire highly qualified individuals that will reduce the need to bloat staff.

Stop operating from a scarcity mindset.

Making effective difference efficiently doesn't mean you should scrimp; it means you need to continually try to improve and reach the next level of excellence. Don't be satisfied with the status quo. Make your vision more audacious! The bigger the vision, the bigger the impact. And ensure that the money moves the needle on that vision becoming a reality.

Unlike a for-profit investment, a donor's return on investment is not monetary. Instead of calculating a percent increase over the dollar amount they gave, you'll want to articulate the good done because of it. If my money isn't doing much good, why would I feel good about giving? If we're no closer to the Promised Land, perhaps we need to re-evaluate our solution, and yes, our overhead.

Stop Begging

I'm sure you've seen children whining for a toy, or candy, or permission to do something their parent is reluctant to allow. The long, drawn-out pleas are enough to make even the most patient saint lose their temper or give in, just to stop the begging.

We know the image conjured in our minds when we hear the word "begging." We know begging when we see it. And who wants to be thought of as a beggar?

Begging is unnerving.

Yet, in some people's minds (board members and staff included), fundraising is begging, and they are uncomfortable with it.

Fundraising isn't begging. Fundraising builds a relationship with a person who cares about what you care about and finds value in your solution to a problem that concerns them. If you can articulate the role the donor plays in solving the puzzle, no begging is involved.

The act of fundraising and the act of giving becomes a joy.

Put simply, when you engage a donor in the vision so they can imagine the value-added to the community, they won't hear begging. They'll want to be involved. They'll feel good about giving because giving feels good, especially when it makes a difference.

Propensity & Capacity

One of the first questions many founders of early-stage nonprofits ask me is, "How do I find donors for my mission?" This question is quickly followed by, "Right now I just have my family and friends, people I know."

Bingo!

You must begin somewhere—and that somewhere is usually in your contact list: your phone, your social media, your business networks. Fundraising for nonprofits usually starts with you and your network. Once you've articulated your Promised Land and how you'll get there, your next step is to consider who you know that has the propensity & capacity to give.

Maybe your mother would give you the shirt off her back. *Propensity.* But she's on a fixed income. *Propensity without capacity.* Perhaps your best friend's brother is a retired dot com millionaire. *Capacity.* Your mission is a pro-choice women's rights organization. That brother is also a deacon in the Catholic church and is fiercely opposed to women's reproductive rights. *Capacity without propensity.*

If you're new to a well-established organization, you may inherit a database full of contacts, some of whom are donors and some who are not. In that case, you'll need to discover more about their propensity and whether they already give at their full capacity. Remember the doctor I visited who'd been contributing $125 annually until I spoke with him, and he gave $10,000.

The fundraising sweet spot comes at the intersection of *propensity* and *capacity.* The key to discovering this sweet spot is communicating. Sure, you can buy a mailing list based on zip code, geographic radius, and public giving records, or scour the donor rolls of other organizations in your industry for names you might recognize. But do you think this cold-call approach will work?

You may learn a bit about these prospects from the information you gather, but the whole thing reminds me of online dating, where you judge a potential match from a snapshot and cursory glance at bio highlights.

Communicate Consistently

We've already talked about the importance of consistent communications for donor cultivation, but it bears repeating here. If you only communicate with donors once or twice a year to ask them for money, you'll likely come across as begging.

Have you ever had a friend, do-gooder, like my friend I call "MIA"? The only time I ever hear from MIA is when she needs something from me. I'm more than happy to help anyone in need if I can. But when I see a missed message, an email, or a social media message from MIA, I know in my gut that she wants something from me. She never asks about me. She never just calls to chat or catch up. I hear from her when she needs something. Otherwise, she is MIA (Missing in Action). Don't be MIA.

I cannot stress enough that one of the most critical aspects of fundraising and developing a fundraising plan is ensuring that you thank donors and report impact abundantly. When you're designing your fundraising plan, make donor stewardship a primary focus. When you're developing job descriptions and evaluative criteria for your fundraising personnel, don't forget to incorporate donor stewardship.

Ask Authentically

Are you old enough to remember the old *Life* cereal commercial where two children push the cereal box between them urging, "you eat it" when they both realize they can ask their friend Mikey instead? "I know, let's ask Mikey." The commercial reminds me of the conversations that often take place in the world of fundraising. Everyone's looking for someone else to give first.

Yeah, do-gooder, I know you work for the organization and probably don't make enough. Or you volunteer and believe that time is money. You're correct. Sharing your time and talent is saving the organization money and costing you something. Your time has value. Hopefully, everyone in the organization shows appreciation and gratitude for these gifts you share. And, hopefully, you experience JOY in the process of giving. In my opinion, giving away money, even a minimal amount, is different.

The truth is, if you don't give before you ask, you may come across as begging. Give first. Before you ever ask another person to give to your organization, donate.

If you can't find it in your heart to donate, asking others to donate seems inauthentic. Not only that, when you give, you become a donor, and then you share that experience with other donors. You understand the donor experience better. In the end, when you give before you ask, you are not asking someone to do what you are unwilling to do first.

The 9th Commandment

Thou shall NOT bear false witness.
Thou SHALL be transparent.

You're doing great work, do-gooder. No doubt. Every day. And hopefully, a do-gooder like you would never purposely, outright, bear false witness—of course, you "don't lie."

Just as stealing is more complicated than monetary theft, not bearing false witness runs much deeper than simply not telling a lie.

At the bare minimum, fundraising demands transactional honesty. We must track and acknowledge all monetary and in-kind donations of time, talent, and treasure and report them accurately as required by law. But since fundraising is more about relationships and impact than about money, it also demands relational honesty—which is where not lying comes even more into play.

As we've discussed all along, do-gooder, you only have so much capacity and so many resources to accomplish everything you hope to do on a given day. Before you develop your fundraising plan, don't forget to allot time for managing both your transactional and relational honesty.

Transactional Honesty

Transactional honesty demands that we promptly provide the legally required documents to our donors and fulfill all local, state, and federal requirements to remain in good standing. Beyond that, we must be fully transparent in all of our transactions.

Does the public have access to view our bylaws, governing documents, policies, and procedures outlining conflict of interest, document retention, and donor privacy standards? Do we publish the agendas and minutes of our board meetings? Do we create job descriptions that honestly outline the expectations for every position—from the board chair and across the organization? Do we post the salary range for every staff position when advertising a position? Do we have expectations that, perhaps unintentionally, exclude the disabled, those from cultures other than the majority, or anyone with learning disabilities that have nothing to do with fulfilling the job requirements?

Transactional honesty is demonstrated by the records we keep, the documents we publish, and the standards to which we hold ourselves and those with whom we choose to conduct business. These transactions take time and resources to establish and maintain. We must commit to implementing transactional honesty so it doesn't become an afterthought because we're too busy raising money to notice or care.

Relational Honesty

The first step of relational honesty in fundraising is to get familiar with the Association of Fundraising Professional's Code of Ethical Standards (afpglobal.org/ethicsmain/code-ethical-standards) and Donor Bill of Rights (afpglobal.org/donor-bill-rights) developed in collaboration with several national organizations.

As a nonprofit organization requesting the general public's support, we have a responsibility to be relationally honest. As we discussed in the 3rd Commandment if we aren't confronting racism in our sector and our community, we are, by default, perpetuating it. When we discuss relational honesty, we cannot ignore the ethical and financial implications of not addressing inclusion and equity issues in our sector.

Inclusion, Diversity, Equity, and Access (IDEA)

While entire books discuss inclusion, diversity, equity, and access (IDEA) in the nonprofit world, any discussion on bearing false witness and relational honesty in fundraising must include thoughts on inclusion, diversity, equity, and access.

The stereotypes, bias, majority norms, white saviorism, and so much of the status quo that makes our society—and many aspects of the social sector tick, are forms of "false witness." Nonprofit leaders have a responsibility to root out the falsehoods attached to so many of the *isms* and phobias that plague society. We cannot claim to be creating a better world when the world we are creating excludes or ignores entire sectors of the population.

A few months ago, I attended a local fundraisers' workshop on IDEA. After exiting the elevator, I had to walk up another flight of stairs. While I had no difficulty with this arrangement, anyone who may have had difficulty climbing stairs would have been unable to attend this meeting.

I'm reasonably certain no one intentionally wanted to exclude anyone from this workshop on inclusion, diversity, equity, and access. And no one told any outright lies. By overlooking the fact that the chosen space was not inclusive, however, the entire conversation about inclusion and access became *false witness*.

- *Leadership*

I pause incredulously when I see women's pregnancy centers with all-male boards and nonprofits working to support communities of color led by an all-white leadership team. While these situations are becoming less frequent, philanthropy can be very lopsided. And until we strengthen the diversity in leadership across the sector, we will continue to bear false witness.

How and where do we seek out board members, donors, and employees? What cultural expectations exist that might make individuals feel less welcome? Do we establish policies and practices that exclude the participation of entire populations? Are our buildings, programs, and services accessible to people with differing physical abilities? Does our board room reflect our community and constituency? From a fundraising perspective, do we allow what wealthy donors might think to dictate who we invite to the table or the programs we offer?

In our search for diversity, we must also avoid tokenism. Do we invite people of color, the disabled, and representatives of marginalized communities to the table simply to check a box, or do we truly value the perspective they bring? Has their presence changed our interactions, or have they needed to adapt to *fit* the majority culture and norms?

- *Language*

Last year, while conducting a strategy session for an organization that empowers physically disabled individuals through access to competitive sport(s) opportunities, I intended the participants to break into groups in different areas of the large room. After posting oversized sticky notes on the walls, I directed everyone to "go stand near the category that most drew their attention." The minute I spoke the word "stand," I realized that half of the people in the room were using wheelchairs. I immediately stopped using the word "stand," and replaced it with "gravitate towards," "find the one," and "move near." No one had called me out. I'm not sure anyone even noticed. But if I genuinely believe words matter, which I do, I needed to recognize the bias in my language and find more respectful options.

Of course, do-gooder, these biases are not limited to the examples of ableism I've shared. They extend to race, ethnicity, religion, gender, sexual identity and orientation, mental health—the list goes on. We must consider if our language is binary in nature, excluding many LGBTQIA+ individuals. Do the registration and donation forms and data management systems we use reflect diverse identities? Are we creating environments of inclusion or exclusion with our event invitations and marketing language? Do we recognize the holidays of one religious tradition more than another? Do we hold expectations of cultural competency that some may not share?

Paying attention to the words we use when talking to and about our neighbors and our non-neighbors (if there's such a thing) is critical to not bearing false witness and building relational honesty.

- *Images*

I recently attended a conference where someone speaking about homelessness in Seattle had a slide presentation filled with African American images. Not even half the population of homeless individuals in Seattle is African American. The percentage difference between the population of African American and white people experiencing homelessness is 9%. The photos were not actual photos of the program participants, and every photo featured African Americans. This is neither transactional nor relational honesty—and it perpetuates racism.

A client once shared their newly designed brochure filled with photos of volunteers reading to children. Every photo except one featured professionally dressed adults reading to children. The only adult Person of Color in the brochure dressed as a blue-collar laborer. When I asked if any professional People of Color volunteered, she informed me these were stock photos, and she just hadn't noticed.

When we develop marketing and fundraising materials, do our communications accurately portray the reality of our cause and the scope of our impact, or do they perpetuate stereotypes?

Beyond the diversity needed in the board room and leadership positions, it is important to recognize when our assumptions, status quo, and lack of awareness perpetuate the falsehoods about and exclusion of any individual or group in our society. The call to not bear false witness against our neighbor means we must be particularly aware of how we show respect and portray the problem we are solving.

While you may think these internal processes have little to do with fundraising, I'd like to assert that everything has to do with fundraising! Because fundraising requires integrity and ethical principles. And if we can't ensure our organization's integrity, how can we guarantee our donors we are acting ethically regarding their contributions?

Relational Honesty with Donors

The Golden Rule states, "Do unto others as you would have them do unto you," or "Don't do to others what you don't want to be done to you." Relational honesty demands that we go beyond the golden rule of treating others how we want to be treated. To practice relational honesty, we must embrace the platinum rule—"Treat others how THEY want to be treated." Discover how donors want to be treated. Then do that.

Connect The Why

Your job, do-gooder, is to listen at least as much as you talk.

Fundraising is a relationship built around a shared vision of the Promised Land. Learn everything you can about your donors and prospective donors. Ask for their opinions. Seek their advice. Understand their catalyst and motivation to understand their vision and share how your mission aligns with theirs.

Each donor has a personal WHY—why they care about one problem, why they favor one solution over another. They hope to reach their Promised Land, to accomplish their vision for a better world, whatever that means to them, through their generosity. If you center WHY in your fundraising efforts, those who share your WHY will want to support you.

Not everyone will care as much about your mission as you do. You might know individuals who have the capacity to give to your organization, but your ONE mission doesn't appeal to them. This doesn't mean your mission isn't valid; you just can't be all things to all people. You chose your mission; every individual must choose theirs. If they have a different Promised Land, don't keep wandering the desert with them. Move on.

- *Create Connection, Offer Opportunity*

People hear and respond to campaigns differently. Once you identify and know where to find your potential donors, converting them to actual donors takes learning to connect. Do you need to tug on their heartstrings or offer clear, concise proof of effectiveness? Are they concerned about your credibility and capacity? Do they want a business-like approach or a more personal touch? Should you reach out to them during the workday or after hours and on weekends? If you don't know the answers to how your donors prefer to connect, ask.

Some folks love a great night out for a worthy cause; others prefer writing a check and calling it a day. While you might love to golf and think inviting others to join a foursome will win them over, you could be missing all those who dread a day on the green. Which opportunities will engage which donors?

- *Personal Visits*

As I've suggested, to manage your fundraising, you'll want to identify those donors who will be cultivated and stewarded on a more personal level than the more mass-market, stadium approach to communications. One of the key features of this personal relationship is individual or small group meetings. Fundraisers typically reserve these meetings for donors who've demonstrated a commitment and a capacity to support the organization at a high level. If you are meeting someone in person, let them know why you want to meet. What is the purpose of the meeting? Do you hope to learn more about what they wish to do with their philanthropy? Are you sharing program updates and success stories, so they know how vital their support is to the mission? Will you ask their opinion about your board's strategic decisions, so they feel more invested in the future?

Remove Yourself from the Equation

Convincing potential supporters to care is not the same as creating a laundry-list of the programs you offer and how many people you serve. When your communications focus only on the great programs and services you provide or how important it is to fulfill your mission, the donor can get lost in the jargon and generalities.

Like my experience with Narcissa, the friend I mentioned earlier, your donor will wonder if their presence is necessary, much less appreciated. If you're already doing such a fantastic job, why do you need me? What part do I play?

Your organization is the facilitator of the relationship between the donor and the person receiving services. Your organization facilitates the services, but that doesn't make you the hero. Remove yourself from the equation. Try not to get in the way. Don't create a false narrative, forgetting the role the donor plays in making good things happen. Let them know the real impact of their gift.

Be transparent

I learned early on from my good Catholic mother and teachers that sins of omission are as sinful as sins of commission. In other words, what we don't say can sometimes be worse than what we do say. If we are committed to relational honesty, then part of not bearing false witness is financial transparency.

Accountability and transparency are now an expectation for businesses, politicians, and nonprofits alike. Savvy donors research and judge organizations before they give. New websites and mobile apps evaluating nonprofit performance based on a wide range of criteria are popping up all the time. Social media has become a platform for both sharing and demanding information about the inner workings of global, national, and even the smallest organizations.

As a nonprofit organization that relies on charitable donations, not bearing false witness means you must be transparent. The public has the right to know where their money is going. And you never want to do anything that makes someone ask, "What do they have to hide?"

Share Policy and Procedure

Despite having raised less than $2000 in their first year, one of my clients created such an impressive annual impact report that it caught the attention of local city and county officials and led to numerous networking and service opportunities. By year two, their revenue increased more than ten-fold, and their organizational impact grew exponentially.

Many of my small and early-stage clients think they are too small or too new to worry about establishing policies and practices around transparency. I say, the sooner, the better.

At the very least, follow the law and file the appropriate Form 990 and create an annual report, however simple. Call it a Gratitude, Impact or Annual Report, or coin another brand-related title. Regardless of the name, the measure of a year well-spent bears witness to the impact of financial donations, in-kind gifts, volunteer hours, and moral support on those you serve.

Include happy and less happy events and expenditures, too. Be honest about your capacity, your impact, and your balance sheet. Don't try to make your organization look like something it isn't – for better or worse. Be honest.

In addition to publishing an annual report and filing your Form 990, adopt and publish policies on your website. Release reports beyond those required by law. Engender trust and confidence among your donors.

Charity Watchdog Groups

Several organizations work to promote transparency and accountability among nonprofits online and via social media. Many private and family foundations use information from these watchdog groups before offering a grant or donating to any nonprofit organization. Be sure to establish and monitor your organization's profiles on these various sites regularly to update information, correct errors, and develop a reputation for transparency and accountability. An internet search could offer many nonprofit rating options, but a few well-known sites include:

- *Candid*

   Candid (which was formed by the merge of GuideStar with Foundation Center in 2019) aggregates information about the mission, programs, operations, and finances of nonprofit organizations, regardless of the size. This information is not judged, rated, or ranked dependent on overhead ratios or program impact. The ranking system, designated by seals, is based on your level of transparency. The more information you provide in your profile, the stronger your organization's Seal of Transparency.

- *Charity Navigator*

   Charity Navigator evaluates 24 metrics related to an organization's finances, accountability, and transparency by analyzing information from their website and Form 990s. Charity Navigator reviews organizations with at least seven years' history, $1m in revenue, and $500K in donations. Charity Navigator has also introduced the Encompass Rating System (in beta at the time of writing) which gives nonprofits a platform to demonstrate their transparency and effectiveness. Organizations scoring 75 or above will receive the "Give with Confidence" designation.

- *Charity Watch*

   Charity Watch works diligently to expose inefficiencies within organizations and grades their spending habits and transparency accordingly.

- *BBB Wise Giving Alliance*

   The *Better Business Bureau* uses 20 standards in governance & oversight, measured effectiveness, finances, fundraising, and informational materials to grade nonprofits.

- *Great Nonprofits*

  Great Nonprofits is the spot where you and your supporters can tell your nonprofit story. You can gather reviews and ratings from the community you serve, like Yelp for nonprofits, and earn a badge to boost donor confidence and potentially increase donations.

When you monitor and update your profiles regularly, you're better positioned to manage your online identity, save time with your grant applications, and increase funding. Monitoring these sites can be an excellent method of engagement for a board member or other volunteer—and save staff time.

Being fully transparent makes fundraising more authentic and is important for building relational honesty. When you practice relational honesty, you invite the potential donor to be an actor in the solution for a problem they care about. Fundraising becomes mutually beneficial. You won't need to beg, your donors won't feel like you're stealing, and you are in no danger of bearing false witness to make a buck.

All the planning in the world falls short if you don't ask. And if you don't ask, you deprive someone who shares your vision of the joy that comes from giving. Go ahead, joy someone.

And if you don't ask, you deprive
someone who shares your vision of the joy
that comes from giving.

Janet Cobb

The 10th Commandment

Thou shall NOT covet others' goods.
Thou SHALL keep calm and fundraise.

Did you hear about the anonymous donor who paid the $4,000,000 mortgage of a historically black church in Georgia? Or the Catholic high school in California that received a $1 million-plus windfall from an investment in Snap Chat?

Wouldn't it be great if every nonprofit had such support? Sure, it would be great; but unfortunately, a wish is not what you can take to the bank. Instead, we do-gooders work and plan and worry about "making budget" to keep our missions going, making sure that as our money burns, our tree is not consumed.

Don't Covet

You hear stories of other organizations bringing in tens of thousands in online campaigns and hundreds of thousands from special events. You read about the millions raised on regional and national giving days and the bequests left behind by quiet, unassuming librarians and janitors. You want what these organizations have, but you can't figure out how to share in their windfall. How do they do it? What is their secret? You think, if only—

If only someone could hand me the perfect fundraising plan; if only my board would ask their rich friends; if only our video would go viral; if only—

Sure, we may not consciously covet what another organization has. To covet is to desire strongly, to lust after or inordinately desire something that belongs to another. But many get lost in "if only" and lust after the quick fix. They want the enormous social media following, the database full of wealthy donors, the mailing list that will guarantee to bring in the big bucks.

Playing the waiting victim rather than making things happen is a recipe for failure. The "if only" attitude is also contrary to the culture of gratitude and the growth mindset we've already discussed.

Another danger lurking near "if only" is the fear of mission out (FOMO). When FOMO drives us, we can get so caught up in not missing an opportunity to "make a buck" that we forget how critical it is to build relationships, honor the donor, and practice relational honesty. Or we try every new social media platform or trendy event, so we don't miss an opportunity. Much like being in a hurry (as we discussed in the 4th Commandment), FOMO can lead to rash, frenzied fundraising that comes off as begging.

The Myth and Danger of Comparisons

Many of my clients are small, early-stage organizations eager to make an impact. They work long hours, expend sweat equity, and give it their all. Some see rabid growth and hit fundraising targets and program success quickly. Others struggle.

Many, whether they struggle or not, wonder how they compare to other organizations. They ask about the size of their contact list, their contact to donor ratio, their email open and click rates, their direct mail return on investment, and their dollars raised. They all want to know, "How do we compare?"

While I'm all for being data-driven and think it is critical to know how your fundraising efforts are performing, I urge caution when worrying too much about national averages and fundraising and communication statistics.

Maybe because years ago, I stopped caring too much about what others think of me or how I "stack up" OR perhaps because statistics can certainly bear false witness— I hesitate to go down the road of comparing one organization's performance to another. Instead, as I hope I taught my children, I urge my clients to compare how they're doing against their established goals and previous years.

Rather than continually comparing their performance to industry benchmarks, I encourage them to develop specific, measurable goals that will become their key performance indicators (KPI). A key performance indicator is a business term for how close you are to achieving your stated goals.

Through the process of strategic planning, you've highlighted the priorities for your organization. With your goals and objectives clearly outlined, you are in a strong position to decide which factors will most impact achieving those goals. You cannot improve everything all at once. Identifying 3-4 KPIs that correlate to your strategic plan's focus areas is critical for moving from a covetous attitude to a strategic growth mindset.

Let's say you're email open rate is lower than the national average. What good does it do to know that? Of course, if you are doing better than average, that might make you feel good—and I love to share this with clients. But will it change anything? Will you not keep trying to reach a higher open rate? Will you settle for the status quo and not do what you can to improve your next email engagement?

While hitting national averages might make you feel good about yourself for a moment, you shouldn't ride the wave for too long. Wouldn't it be better to compare your own emails' open rates to consider what might be influencing them? Could it be the subject line, time of day, day of the week?

As I reviewed the open rates of recent communications with one of my clients, we noticed the open rate increased any time their subject line offered some humor. When they made any mention of needing money, the open rate dropped. Another client noticed the open rate increased whenever they clearly stated that they needed support in the subject line. The point here, do-gooder, is that every community is unique. You would do better to understand your own and strive to improve your engagement than to compare yourself to another organization.

That said, KPIs can help you see your progress when you feel stuck on the treadmill. KPIs demonstrate the progress you might forget or completely overlook.

KPIs can also provide information to create realistic budget goals, complete grant applications and reports, and let major donors and corporate or foundation funders know that you understand data. Having critical numbers on hand if someone asks makes you more credible and keeps you accountable to those who support your mission. And ultimately, understanding your KPIs will help you strategize to achieve your vision more effectively and efficiently.

If you aren't hitting your KPIs, you might need new

Total expense ÷ Total raised = Fundraising ROI

---

fundraising tactics. For example, if your KPI is to increase the number of your recurring donors by 10% in one year, and you don't hit that mark, you'll need to ask yourself why. What did you do, or not do, that would have influenced your ability to hit that mark?

- *Fundraising ROI*

One KPI many organizations track is the Fundraising ROI or Cost to Raise a Dollar, which is an excellent reminder that you want to prepare for profitability (3rd Commandment). While making money is not the goal for a nonprofit organization, every organization is wise to monitor mission progress against the bottom line. To better understand the cost-effectiveness of each fundraising effort, I recommend that you review your revenue streams and expenses in segments according to tactic. What is the cost to secure a gift through direct mail, email, special events, major gifts, and planned giving?

If your mailing costs $1200 to prepare and send (be sure to consider staff preparation time) and you only bring in $800, you've lost money. Should you not send the mailing? Could you reduce the expense by not sending as many? One organization I worked with sent four appeals a year to 22,000 alumni for more than ten years and only ever received return gifts from fewer than 200. I don't remember the financial numbers, but clearly, they had room to reduce the mailing size. If someone hadn't responded in that many years, they weren't likely to react suddenly unless something drastic changed. On the other hand, the school could reduce expenses and increase their investment return with a few simple changes.

- *Donor Growth*

Knowing if your donor revenue is growing or if you're gaining new donors each year can give you insight into how you're doing, not just financially. Of course, it is crucial to understand what's happening with your donor base. If you had 100 donors last year, you hopefully have at least 100 or more donors this year. And if you raised

---

Donor Growth Rate = ((2019 donors − 2018 donors) ÷ 2018 donors) × 100

Donation Growth Rate = ((2019 donations − 2018 donations) ÷ 2018 donations) × 100

$50,000 last year, hopefully, you'll raise more this year. Calculating that growth is not difficult as long as you know your numbers. For a 2018 to 2019 comparison, you would subtract 2018 from 2019, divide by 2018 and multiply by 100.

The bigger question here is, "What led to the growth or decline?" Did something happen in one year and not in another? Is that event repeatable or preventable? Did you engage or communicate differently? Can you proactively do anything to buck or continue a trend? What will you add to your fundraising plan to positively impact the growth rate?

- *Donor Retention Rate*

In addition to your growth rate, you'll want to track your donor retention rate. Donor or revenue growth doesn't mean you've maintained strong relationships with your donors. You could have lost donors but acquired new ones. Or fewer donors may have given larger gifts. Or more donors may have contributed smaller gifts. Knowing your donor retention rate allows you to understand better if you're building relationships with donors or merely

---

Exact retention:
   (# of donors who gave last year and this year ÷ # of
      those same donors who gave last year) x 100
General retention:
   (# of donors this year ÷ # of donors last year) x 100

---

receiving occasional gifts from somewhat random donors.

Count how many donors you had last year; then find how many of those _same_ donors gave again this year. You retained those donors. Then divide this year by last year. That is your donor retention rate.

- *Communication Engagement*

Understanding how engaged your supporters are with your communications can be challenging. We have no idea what happens when someone receives our direct mail piece unless they return a gift in the envelope we provide. We can't know if those who didn't use the return envelope ignored our communication, read it, and actively decided not to contribute, or planned to donate but forgot.

Your email communication provides a clearer picture. And examining the open, click, and conversion rates of your current, lapsed, and prospective donors will help you create messages that resonate. You can avoid landing in the spam folder by using an organizational email to distribute your email blasts and by asking those who sign up for your e-news to add your organization's email to their contact list. Adding social sharing buttons to your emails can increase your click-through rates. Using personalized emails can improve your click-rates and your conversion rates. If you include links to videos, articles, or other websites, you will learn more about your community members' interests. And when you send surveys and polls asking for feedback and insights, you discover even more. Don't be afraid to understand what your community wants.

Average Open Rate – 25.96%
Average Click Rate – 3.05%
Emails sent to spam – 12%
Social sharing buttons increase click rate – 158%
Personalized email increase click rate – 14%
Emails opened on mobile devices – 53%
Sending 4 emails per month increases open rate

*https://www.causevox.com/blog/6-nonprofit-email-marketing-stats

---

- *How many are too many?*

Traditional research shows that a person needs to hear a message seven times before it registers, but some are now saying, in this digital age, that number triples to 21 times. Think of the advertising strategies of for-profit companies.

How are you cutting through the noise? Is your message being heard?

Most organizations do not communicate enough.

Some of the largest organizations send monthly mailings with emails in between – because it works for them. Others have learned that open and click rates and donations increase when an organization sends weekly instead of monthly emails.

Remember, you are not your donor – and many studies have shown that what might bother you or your board is not going to impact your donor base in the same way.

I can hear you now, "But what about donor fatigue?" or "Won't they unsubscribe?"

My response: Those who care about what you care about want to know what's going on. Frequency is not likely the culprit. Content is. If folks unsubscribe, as the saying goes, "they really aren't that into you."

That said, have a compelling reason to invade my inbox. Keep my interest piqued. Share stories of success. Be vulnerable in the face of failure. Rile me to anger when appropriate. Remember, if your communications read like nutrition labels, why would anyone want to hear from you. If you get this right, your donors will love to hear from you.

Best Practices

Along the same lines as benchmarks and KPIs is the question of best practices. While I always encourage clients to follow best practices, I still believe there are many ways to do life—and fundraising. Sure, do-gooder, there are best practices. Best practices are those techniques and habits that most commonly lead to success. That doesn't mean if you don't follow best practices, you'll completely fail or that following them will lead to guaranteed success in every situation. Sometimes what works for others won't work for your circumstances.

The takeaway is that you aren't alone in doing this kind of work, do-gooder. Learn what you can from the experiences of others. Do everything you can to learn from others who came before you, who've already made mistakes, who've been at this nonprofit work longer than you. Understand what others are saying works or doesn't.

Always strive to do better to provide impactful programs and services, craft meaningful communications, and build relationships with donors. But don't compare your success to others', and don't covet what others have. Compare only to yourself so you do better with every passing day.

And, when it comes to best practices, don't let the desire to be perfect get in the way of giving others the opportunity to do good. Some do-gooders get so caught up with the fear of not communicating or fundraising perfectly. Reality is, you can only start and work with who you are, who you know, and what you have. So, do that! And, as you make mistakes, apologize when appropriate, and learn from them. Do your best to do better.

Don't Compete

A close cousin to comparing to others is competing with them. Too many small nonprofits concerned about raising the funds they need for their mission act like fundraising is a competition. Accustomed to a scarcity mentality, some do-gooders feel like they need to hoard their donors so another nonprofit doesn't *snatch* them. The truth is, those who contribute to one organization may contribute to another. Philanthropic donors often donate to several organizations that address a similar cause or to several different causes they care about.

You don't need to worry about what other causes or organizations a donor supports. You simply need to know if your mission moves them. Do they care about the problem you are solving? Do they believe in your solution? If another organization shares its mission with a donor who chooses to make a gift, they haven't stolen your donor. They've simply provided the donor with another opportunity to experience the joy of giving and positively impact one cause they care about in the world.

On that note, competition for donors and resources within the nonprofit arena can also perpetuate systemic inequity. We would all do better to search for ways to collaborate and uplift other organizations working in our community or our mission focus area. As the old saying goes, "a rising tide lifts all boats." Rather than compete, let's work together to celebrate our community's strengths and work to ensure no one is left behind.

And don't worry, do-gooder, there is plenty of money to go around!

Keep Calm and Fundraise

I've met with more than one founder chasing $100,000, $350,000, and even $1 million goals to meet an arbitrary annual budget when they've yet to demonstrate impact with a minimum viable product or raise funds from anyone but their closest friends and relatives.

I'd like to think they are zealous for their cause and will quickly learn the time it takes to build meaningful, lasting relationships. Unfortunately, early-stage nonprofits aren't alone in setting arbitrary fundraising goals despite their current reality.

During a recent call, a client shared that the board had just handed down the expected fundraising goal for the year—at more than double the previous year's goal. Their desire to maintain quality services led to the new goal, but they offered no insight into how to accomplish this doubling of income.

Too many nonprofit development and finance committees base fundraising goals on their expenses instead of on the reality of their current and potential donor base. Others believe you should budget a percentage increase year over year, even when you don't meet the previous year's goal. They often expect unrealistic and impossible results from directors of development and wonder why the average turn-around for development directors is 18 months.

Fundraising Plan vs. Fundraising Campaign

I like to differentiate between a fundraising plan and a fundraising campaign with a few key points. For me, the fundraising plan is the overarching itinerary that drives all your fundraising activities throughout the year. In contrast, a fundraising campaign is one set of activities with a particular goal. Your campaign is more like one leg of the trip. And the various elements of the campaign are the turn-by-turn navigation that will get you to your destination. In other words, your fundraising plan might include numerous campaigns with distinct goals and objectives. To be most effective, create the overarching fundraising plan and then further outline each campaign's details.

Your fundraising plan will include your approach to securing grants, corporate partnerships, planned gifts, major gifts, annual giving, and monthly giving programs. Your plan will cover personal solicitation, direct mail, email and social media campaigns, and special events. You'll outline your financial goals for each approach. Your plan will cover the entire year and include every element of each campaign so that, just like in your communications plan, you can see the bigger picture.

On the other hand, your fundraising campaign will outline all of the elements, the timeline, and the channels you will use to raise money within a given timeframe for a particular purpose and from specific groups. You may have three or four fundraising campaigns a year, or you might have twelve.

Sample Fundraising

Campaign Dates	Who	Strategy	Number to be Solicited	Target Ask Amount	Average Gift Size	Total Revenue	Associated Expenses	Net Income	Non-monetary Goal
	Board Member Commitments		$	$		$	$	$	
	Individual Donors (below $1000)					Estimated Income	Associated Expenses	Net Income	
	Current Donors		$	$		$	$	$	
	Lapsed Donors		$	$		$	$	$	
	Prospective Donors		$	$		$	$	$	
	Major Donors (above $1000)					Estimated Income	Associated Expenses	Net Income	
	Current Donors		$	$		$	$	$	
	Lapsed Donors		$	$		$	$	$	
	Prospective Donors		$	$		$	$	$	
	Monthly Recurring Donors (below $1000)					Estimated Income	Associated Expenses	Net Income	
	Current Donors		$	$		$	$	$	
	Lapsed Donors		$	$		$	$	$	
	Prospective Donors		$	$		$	$	$	
	Special Events	Strategy	Number to be Invited	Sponsorship Levels	Ticket Price	Estimated Income	Associated Expenses	Net Income	
	Event Name		$	$		$	$	$	
	Event Name		$	$		$	$	$	
	Private and Government Foundations	Program Officer	Date of Meeting with PO/Liaison	Target Ask Amount	Average Anticipated Award	Estimated Income	Associated Expenses	Net Income	
	Foundation/Agency name		$	$	$	$	$		
	Foundation/Agency name		$	$	$	$	$		
	Foundation/Agency name		$	$	$	$	$		
	Foundation/Agency name		$	$	$	$	$		

For example, one element of your annual plan might be to increase monthly recurring donors by 5%. You may decide to run three campaigns: one in January, one in May, and one in August. You might direct each campaign to a different audience: one to lapsed donors, one to non-donors, and one to current donors who you hope to convert to monthly donors. You may also decide to use three communication channels for each campaign: email, snail-mail, and phone calls.

As you can see, your fundraising campaigns are much more detailed and targeted than your overarching fundraising plan. My encouragement to you, do-gooder, is to outline each campaign as you create your fundraising plan so you're able to right-size the plan to fit your capacity to implement. You cannot give full attention to making phone calls to request current donors become monthly donors the same week you're expected to complete the grant reports for two program grants and host a special event for your major donors.

Fundraising is a Contact Sport

I like to say fundraising is a contact sport. Not so much two teams slamming into one another to stop progress, like in football or hockey. More like the quarterback in American football. A great quarterback understands his offensive unit. They practice together, understand one another's moves, run plays, and root for one another—all before game day. On game day, it all comes together, and they effectively carry the ball into the opponent's end zone.

As the old football saying goes, "Any given Sunday." On any given Sunday, a football team could lose. No two Sundays are alike. The better the quarterback and offensive team communicate and understand one another, the more likely they are to score touchdowns and win the game.

The same holds for fundraising. Like the quarterback, you must engage. The more contact you make with donors outside of the ask, the better your chances of accomplishing your goal to change the world together. You need to prepare for all eventualities, and you can't be afraid to lose. No one wins all the time. But if you're sending off fundraising communications or heading into prospective donor meetings without doing your homework and learning and listening to what matters to your donor, you're likely to fail.

Don't get me wrong. You'll hear "no, not yet, and maybe" often enough, regardless of your training and preparation—any given Sunday. As the old fundraising saying goes, "If you don't hear "NO" two to three times a week, you aren't asking enough." But when you go in prepared, you'll begin to hear "yes" more often.

Like contact sports, fundraising takes training and preparation before you make contact. If you never make contact, you're not in the game. If you're afraid or ill-prepared to make contact, you'll never win. If you make all your fundraising plays from behind your desk, you're riding the bench and won't make the first string. If you make no contact, fundraising doesn't happen.

While you can't survive with no donors and you need diverse revenue streams, when it comes to building donor relationships, begin with those you know: your community, your people, and your audience (See the 5th Commandment). Too often, the "more" attitude drives fundraising efforts. More, more, more. More social media followers and likes. More names in the database. More people at more fundraising events. Everyone is looking for more—believing more is better. More isn't necessarily better. Spending too many resources, trying to find more prospective donors is often time-consuming and ineffective.

Wouldn't it be best to have a few terrific friends you enjoy spending time with, trust, and know you can count on? Isn't one good friend better than ten acquaintances?

Donors to your nonprofit are the same. One engaged, reliable, committed donor is better than ten or a hundred not-so-committed, unreliable social media followers or sporadic donors. Of course, with a robust three-plan approach in place, you will hopefully convert some of these not-so-committed folks to become avid, impactful donors.

Who's in the Game?

- *Donor Retention*

Securing a second or subsequent donation from someone who has donated once is more likely, more important, and less expensive than continually searching for new donors. When planning your fundraising, begin by asking how you're treating your current and previous donors. When they gave a gift, did they feel appreciated? Have you made sure they know how much their contribution means to your organization and the cause? How many times do you make contact between the transactional receipt and the next ask? Do you only reach out to ask for money like my friend MIA? Do you treat donors like your ATM?

Put yourself in their shoes. If you were them, would you be excited to give again? Would you feel like many parents do when their kids only reach out when they need money?

Building a relationship with donors takes time and resources. You need to decide how best to use the resources you have, but if you do nothing else, do-gooder, revisit your approach to donor retention. (Review the Culture of Gratitude section of the 5th Commandment)

- *Donor Upgrades*

My grad school alma mater called me regularly for years, asking for a gift. For various reasons, this institution was not high on my list of philanthropic causes. One year, about four years ago, I gave a small year-end gift before deciding, for various reasons, that I would never make a gift to that institution again. During a recent phone-a-thon, the student enlisted to call me requested more than five times the amount of my previous, small one-time gift. Five times!

I expressed surprise at the ask amount and informed the caller that I was not interested in ever donating to the institution again. The young lady politely asked me why and listened sympathetically to my concerns about recent administrative decisions that had negatively impacted my family. When I finished my explanation, she made another request for half the original ask amount! I'll not bore you with the continuing details of what ended up being a long conversation, but I will point out that when considering requesting a donor upgrade, be sure to right-size the ask. And when a donor says they will never give again, don't keep asking for different amounts!

Remember the doctor I mentioned in the 5th commandment? The one who'd given $125 for 20 years to his high school alma mater and one discussion led to a $10,000 scholarship. He'd said, "No one ever asked me."

Most nonprofits don't ask often enough, in the right way, for the appropriate amount, or at the appropriate moment in the cultivation cycle. Donor upgrade needs to be rooted in relational honesty rather than transactional begging.

- Ask *their vision* of the Promised Land. Don't focus on your need but help them understand the power and impact of a larger gift in creating the world they desire. Explain what difference a larger gift will make.

- Ask *more often*. Rather than sending only one letter a year at the gift date anniversary or at year-end or because it is Giving Tuesday or some other philanthropy day, consider sending additional requests throughout the year. We're all concerned about donor fatigue. But if we've engaged with donors more than just when we ask for money, they are not as likely to feel donor fatigue. They will support the cause they care about when the need is presented.

- Ask for a *stretch gift*. At certain times, opportunities present themselves to ask for a stretch gift. During a specific program expansion, capital campaign, or on an anniversary year for the organization, you can ask for an added amount above and beyond their usual gift as a short-term increase in giving. A stretch gift like this may or may not lead to continued larger contributions but is one way to invite a donor to have a greater impact.

▪ Ask for a *monthly gift*. Monthly gifts help with both personal and organizational cash flow. Cash flow expands impact. When you don't need to find ways to make ends meet continually, your energies go elsewhere. Don't get me wrong. You need to continue to cultivate those relationships, but you've moved into a different phase of the relationship. Don't ignore them. Their gifts are "automatic," but your gratitude should not be. Don't bombard them with continuous appeals, convincing them of the value of the vision. They're already walking with you to the Promised Land. But don't be afraid to ask for additional gifts (especially when you have a challenge grant, are very close to a specific campaign goal, or on a giving day).

▪ Ask for *non-cash gifts*, when appropriate. These can be in the form of stocks, insurance, securities, vehicles, or property.

• *Donor Acquisition*

I recently met with a new board member for a client organization to discuss a communications project. This new board member had been volunteering with the organization for almost ten years and turned in high-capacity circles. When I mentioned the annual appeal letter that would be part of the project, she looked dumbfounded. In her ten years as a volunteer, she had never received an appeal. They'd never asked her for a gift.

Sometimes, acquiring new donors is simply seeing what is right in front of you.

Another newly appointed office manager turned executive director of a 25-year-old faith-driven community theater company wondered how she'd ever find new supporters. Working only part-time and responsible for all operations and marketing, she felt stuck behind the desk keeping the wheels turning. When she finally began to attend local events for business and nonprofit leaders and shared her vision for the future, others who shared her vision seemed to come out of the woodwork. In just a few months, they've created new partnerships, expanded programs, and developed an exciting vision for the community. Sometimes you have to get out and about to find your People.

Sometimes you need to invite them to come to you. These invitations might come through introductions from your community; through engagement on social media; or through an event that introduces new folks to your mission and vision. These events don't need to be major fundraising events. They can be as simple as an open house or small gathering at the home of a board member—as long as we aren't in the middle of a pandemic.

Regardless of where and how you go about finding new donors, don't forget that fundraising is about building relationships, not just about getting people to give you a buck. These initial points of engagement are just that—a point of first contact.

Finally, let's not forget the power of technology. With the phenomenal technological tools at our fingertips, we

---

Sometimes acquiring new donors is simply seeing what is right in front of you.

---

can acquire new donors without ever meeting someone in person. Contact can happen on crowdfunding sites, through peer-to-peer campaigns, via social media, and through email.

What Should You Say?

- *Individual Giving*

The we-centric approach of writing appeals to prove you are worthy of a donor's money is likely the result of the grant writing process. Grantors often rely on proof of concept, credibility, and organizational capacity to distinguish how their money will have the greatest impact when deciding who will receive grants.

When seeking donations from individual donors, this we-centric approach can be detrimental. Think for a minute of *Go Fund Me* and other social giving, crowdfunding websites where people in need ask for money. The individuals who share stories of unpaid medical bills, unaffordable funeral expenses for a loved one gone too soon, or unexpected legal fees to fight unjust treatment don't have 501c3 status. They don't have a full spectrum of programs and services, impact reports, and a history of proper reporting. They simply share their stories. And people give them money.

No one who supports these individuals receives a tax deduction. These folks don't give for a tax deduction, high-impact program results, or the low overhead. Thousands of dollars pass through these platforms because one person's story moves another person to act.

Individual donor giving is not grant-writing. A grant-giving entity balances numerous nonprofits' requests and wants to ensure grantees will spend their money wisely.

They're trying to identify the organizations that will give them the biggest bang for their buck. Their decisions, for this reason, need to be more calculated and strategic. They often have hundreds of applications for a minimal number of grants. Individual donors are not committees weighing the pros and cons of a proposal against hundreds of other potential recipients. Passion for a cause or a solution drives most individual donors to give. An individual donor wants to make another person's or animal's life or a community's situation better. Whether you provide crisis, crucial, or cultural services, philanthropy is about the love of people.

People give to people. For this reason, you'll need to gather the stories of people. People who work in your organization. People who volunteer. People who are impacted by your solution and their families and friends.

Some organizations resist the notion that we can ask individuals who participate in programs to contribute financially. I'd disagree. As someone who received the charitable services of many organizations throughout most of my life, I know two things: I never got upset when I received the appeals from those organizations, even when I wasn't in a position to donate; and, when I was in a place to donate, I gladly gave to those organizations that had helped me along the way. I can't speak for everyone, but I believe we can't judge others' wallets or hearts. As my mother taught me each year when she handed a canned good to contribute to the food drive at school, "There may be someone worse off than we are." We invite; we don't judge.

- *Give Me One Good Reason*

Not every ask needs to explain EVERYTHING you do. Don't overwhelm the reader with every possible program detail. You can highlight one element but write in such a way that allows for unrestricted gifts. Sharing a story about how one family facing homelessness needs housing, for example, does not automatically preclude the funds raised through that appeal from being used in another program area of the organization. You can add a word or phrase to indicate donations will support this and other mission programs.

If you can explain how a designated amount of money has an impact, do it. For example, "Your gift of $35 today shelters a homeless teen for a week." You don't need to go into the details of what "shelters" means. This $35 can include paying for electricity, maintenance, washing sheets, or the salaries needed to get this work done. Most people aren't interested in those details, and if anyone is interested, they can request budget details or research your Form 990 on a site like Guidestar.

- *Non-donor asks*

If you contact folks who have never given to your organization, avoid thanking them for their generosity and support. If you thank non-donors, they get the warm fuzzies the brain excretes when we receive gratitude and praise – but they still haven't done what we want them to do—give. And a non-donor might feel like you don't know them or your supporters if you are thanking them for something they've never done.

Instead, create a sense of how good they will feel when they give. Get them excited about the impact they can have when they give. Spark empathy so the personal story of the person in need becomes the non-donor's story. Like a good piece of art, personal circumstances become a universal experience.

- *Writing an appeal letter*

Writing an appeal is unlike all the other writing you'll do throughout the year. For some, this can be terrifying. Remember that you should write from the heart to share with others who care about what you care about, to let them know of an unmet need that they have the opportunity to address. An unmet need does not mean your writing needs to be morose or depressing. You can share a range of emotions telling the story—just as you would in real life when talking to a friend. Write freely and honestly. You'll return to edit at the end, so don't be afraid to get started.

  - To frame the purpose of your letter and get straight to the point, begin by completing the sentence, "I'm writing to you today because…." You don't need to write this phrase out but pencil it in if it helps you focus. The donor will know quickly WHY you're writing to them. Don't send mixed messages.
  - Beginning – tell a story
  - Middle – foster empathy by connecting the story to the reader's story
  - Call to Action – Tell them what to do and avoid words like "partner, help, support."
    - 50¢ a day feeds a child before bedtime.
    - $25 a month shelters a homeless teen for the night.
    - $100 means one more child will gain self-confidence through dance.

- With your donation today, _____ is possible.
- End – remind the donor how their generosity changes the ending of the beneficiary's story. Use action verbs to describe what donations DO. What is their money doing: educating, feeding, preserving, warming, empowering?
- If you wrote the phrase, "I'm writing to you today because," you may consider erasing it.
- Count the "we" vs. the "you" and rewrite sentences to make them donor-focused.
- Once you've written the letter, check that it passes the CUTE test:
  - *Compelling* (C): How critical is the need? How serious is the problem?
  - *Urgent* (U): Why now? Can I respond later?
  - *Targeted* (T): Write to one individual about another individual's predicament
  - *Emotional* (E): Incite empathy, not sympathy. Balance the pain with the hope of resolution.

- *Write the P.S.: The Final Call to Action*

The P.S. in fundraising appeal letters is critical to letting the reader know what to do. From a graphic design perspective, the P.S. draws the reader's eye—often when they will not read any other part of an appeal letter. Studies have shown that including a P.S. will likely increase the number and amount of donations. If your P.S. calls the reader to act, they may donate even without reading the letter.

Much like a book, the first and last lines of any fundraising communication are critical. The opening line needs to draw the reader in and help them understand how vital they are to the ONE mission. The final line drives their response. What should they do in response to everything you've shared in the letter? How can they make a difference? What is the call to action? If they've already read a compelling story giving them a reason to act and explains how their actions will positively impact another person or the world, the P.S. is the final nudge.

- *Check your Cover:*

Despite the admonition to never judge a book by its cover, when it comes to donor communications, the "cover" matters. You can write the best darn communication in the world, but if no one opens it, your masterpiece is worthless. Your package (direct mail envelope or email subject line) needs to catch the eye, pique the interest, and elicit a response.

- *Make Donors Feel Successful*

If you announce a fundraising goal, make sure it's within reach of your donor base, not driven by your budget deficit. Base your goal on the size of your community and audience and their capacity to give. Of course, you don't want to sell yourself short, and you can be happily surprised by blowing through a goal, but generally speaking, you want to help donors feel successful.

- *Set an achievable goal*

The board of a small-town organization launched a campaign in conjunction with a local bakery that offered 50% off the purchase of specially prepared cupcakes if a customer showed proof of a $5 donation to the organization. While some donors would certainly give more than the minimum, a 50% discount on bakery items was not likely to generate too many $5 gifts in this small town. On their online giving page, however, they set a $5,000 fundraising goal. Even for the best bakery items in town, the likelihood of 1000 people donating to this organization in two weeks was slim to none.

- *Enlist initial gifts*

When you create an online giving page, enlist a few donors to start the giving before your page goes live via social media or email blasts. The first few gifts are often the toughest. If I visit a page that wants to raise $100,000, but they haven't received any money, are only a little, I'm likely to think my $25 isn't making a difference. But if you're raising $2500 and $1500 is already raised, I'm happy to pitch in.

- *Offer a match challenge*

Turn to your higher-gift donors, board members, or a foundation to challenge your community to raise funds together through a matching grant. Everyone likes to get more bang for their buck. When you can tell a potential donor their dollar will be doubled with a matching gift, they are more likely to give, even if they can only contribute $10. And higher-end donors might feel better knowing their contribution can be leveraged to encourage others' philanthropy.

- *Make Giving Easy for the Donor*

Write a clear and straightforward call to action. If you are using direct mail, provide clear instructions for giving by mail and online—and include a return envelope. Ensure the font and spacing on all of your direct mail are clear and easy to read, and not too small! If you can personalize the remittance piece so the donor doesn't need to write out their name and contact information, even better.

Giving is an emotional response to a compelling story. Don't make your donor overthink. Tell them exactly what you need them to do.

You may not be old enough to remember the old Tootsie Pop commercials from the 1970s, but in them, a child approached a *Wise Old Owl* to find out how many licks it took to get to the Tootsie Roll center of a Tootsie Pop. The owl licked three times: 1, 2, 3, and bit into the candy, revealing the Tootsie Roll center. "Three licks," he declared.

My slogan for online giving is "1-Click. It takes 1-click to give you my money." A donor should not need to search too hard or click too many times to give you money. When you create your website or online giving pages, ask yourself, "How many clicks?" How many clicks does it take to donate to your nonprofit? When I click the donate button, which should be very easy to find, do I go directly to a donation form to submit my payment information? Or do I land on yet another page explaining various whys for and how-tos of giving?

- *Test your online processes*

Have you tested your systems or asked a family member or friend to do so? Sign-up for your organization's email list. Is it easy to join your email list? Are the benefits of signing up clear? What happens once I submit my email address? Do I get a welcome message sent to my inbox? Do your emails look good on my mobile device? Make a gift. Can I text-to-give? What happens when I make a gift online? Do I get a confirmation receipt for tax purposes? Will I receive a thank you?

Don't Cry Wolf

A private, faith-based school I once worked with recently closed its doors. About ten years ago, the school had made local headlines when the principal camped out on the roof as a fundraising stunt, meant to "save the school." We see these last-ditch efforts pop up in the news from time to time. Alumni, current families, and community members rallied around, and hundreds of thousands of dollars poured in, understanding that they were paying off the mortgage so the school would own their building outright. Then within ten years, the school faced another financial crisis. What happened?

Rather than paying off the mortgage, the board used the money to pay operational expenses and had quietly decided to sell the school building with a ten-year rent-free lease agreement. They'd misled their stakeholders, continued to overspend and made no plans for what would happen next. When the rent-free lease expired, the school had nowhere to turn for support. Nothing they'd done, technically, was illegal; but very few donors wanted to be fooled again.

When you are not facing an unprecedented crisis, sending deficit-funding appeals asking donors to "help us meet our budget" is not the best practice for raising money. Besides being uninspiring and not making the donor feel like a hero, announcing your budget shortfall could leave many prospective donors concerned about your fiscal responsibility. Sharing how a donation changes an individual's life trajectory is far more effective than focusing on a budget shortfall.

Deficit fundraising is never a great idea, but occasionally, you can't avoid it. At these critical moments, be careful to present facts and figures openly and honestly. Don't embellish and don't over-promise and under-deliver.

When Crisis Hits

Just weeks after I completed the first draft of this book, COVID-19 hit. Many clients scrambled to cancel, postpone, or transform planned events. Others faced unimaginable increases in the request for services. Still, others had to shut down their in-person programs, which led to significant revenue loss.

Crisis fundraising is not deficit fundraising. A crisis like COVID-19 or a natural disaster may throw you into a budget deficit, but this is not the same as deficit fundraising. Emergencies like these are totally outside of your control, unexpected, and potentially catastrophic. They are not the result of poor planning or failure to meet goals.

Remember, people want to help people. As I've seen for many clients in 2020, many individuals respond in a crisis. When a crisis hits, your fundraising must be urgent, authentic, and vulnerable. Be honest with the impact the emergency has had on your ability to provide services. Tell your community, your people, and your audience what you need. Their generosity will likely astound, inspire, and humble you.

Creating a Fundraising Plan

Fundraising can be one of the most fulfilling aspects of nonprofit work.

Your strategic plan creates a mission-centric focus. Your communication plan maps out how you will communicate the WHY to those who care about what you care about, with donor-centric communications. Now you can stop raising money in vain, stop begging, and avoid *go away money* by adopting a comprehensive, data-driven fundraising plan. The fundraising plan becomes a practical, tactical approach to acquiring the resources you need to fulfill the vision.

The essential element of a fundraising plan is the commitment to develop an annual plan and to prioritize the resources needed to accomplish it.

Let me say that another way.

If you write a plan but then allow detours and distractions to keep you from implementing it, you've wasted your time. You need to allocate resources, and when necessary, you may need to make sacrifices in other areas of organizational operations. Barring major, unforeseen roadblocks, honor your itinerary. If you don't make fundraising a priority in this way, it can be the most daunting and draining part of nonprofit work.

Once your leadership team commits to developing and prioritizing an annual fundraising plan, you're already halfway to your goal because you already have a clear case for support and the resources you'll need to engage in meaningful conversation with those who care about what you care about.

Step 1. Revisit Your Revenue Streams

When developing a fundraising plan, consider the variety of resources for bringing in revenue to your organization. Which are the most easily accessible for you? Which offers the highest return on investment of time and talent? Can you secure contracts for services? Should you implement service fees? Would in-kind donations provide meaningful support? Are any grant opportunities being ignored?

Step 2. Determine Your Goal from Current Reality

Before beginning your fundraising plan, consider these questions:

- Has everyone in leadership donated monetarily?
- What is the cumulative total of board and leadership giving?
- How many contacts do we have?
- How many donors do we currently have?
- How much have we raised in the past 365 days?
- What is the average gift amount?
- What is the largest gift amount?
- What is our donor retention rate?
- How many lapsed donors do we have? Can we re-engage them?
- Do we know anyone else with the propensity to give?
- What capacity do non-donors have?

When you've gathered the answers to these questions, you have a better picture of your current reality. And from this reality, you should build your plan. If you base your plan on your budget deficit rather than your current reality, you will struggle to reach your goals.

Step 3. Compare Your Goal

Find an industry-standard gift table to see the high-low range of gifts and the number of donors you might need to reach your goal. (For example, giftrangecalculator.com) How does your network of family, friends, and current donors compare to the top-level donor category? Do you know anyone who has both the capacity and propensity to give at the top levels? If so, how many? For every gift, you should anticipate a 1:5 ratio. Securing one $1000 gift means you'll need five people to ask. Review each tier until you can identify the target top-level gift range at which you can name at least five potential donors with whom you have a connection. Adjust the entire table to then account for your top-level amount, with the hopes of getting one or two gifts in that range. Remember the 80/20 (or 90/10) rule. With the top tier you've identified, what would the remainder of your giving capacity look like?

Step 4. Articulate Your Channels

When creating your fundraising plan, you will need to decide what tactics you will employ to engage with returning or new donors to raise the desired revenue. You can write grants, hold special events, send direct mail, launch email and social media campaigns, make phone calls, conduct a peer-to-peer campaign, or make a personal ask. You'll need to articulate how many of each, when, and how you'll implement and manage these various campaigns.

- *Grants Program*

Do you have grant opportunities that might cover the highest levels in the giving table? If so, fantastic! Allocate the time and resources you'll need to apply for and manage those grants. If you're an early-stage nonprofit, be aware that many foundations hesitate to offer grants to organizations with fewer than three years of experience and without specific minimum budgets. Also, remember that the turn-around time for grants can be long. You might begin the process of applying for a grant and not receive funds until a year later.

- *Corporate Partnerships*

Building a corporate giving program takes time and resources. Cold calling or direct mail to local corporations are rarely useful. Board members often play a role in introducing colleagues and friends with corporate ties to your organization. Knowing your board members' networks and understanding their willingness to make these connections on behalf of the organization will go a long way in moving your corporate partnership program forward. If your executive director or a staff member is responsible for forging these partnerships, allocate plenty of time in your fundraising plan. These partnerships rarely bare fruit quickly.

- *Special events: virtual or in-person*

Can you hold a special event that will provide income at a certain level in the gift range table? While I've never recommended too much reliance on them, the 2020 pandemic has taught us to be careful with special events. That said, some events are appropriate and dependable. We don't need to exclude them from our fundraising plan altogether but be sure they are just one piece of a more extensive fundraising program.

Articulate if your event will focus on donor acquisition, donor retention, or donor upgrade? Many people will insist they are doing all three, but your event is likely to be less effective in all three areas if that's the case. You only have so much time and can only be interacting with so many prospective donors at one time (even if many people are involved in the process). Decide what your primary goal will be and do that well.

Are you looking for a quick influx of cash at a specific time of year? Could you offer a niche event catering to folks who appreciate an activity, like a 5K, golf outing, trivia night, or comedy show? Attendees may be more interested in the activity than your cause, but they'll come for the fun. Remember, these types of events are not likely to result in donor acquisition unless you work deliberately to convert an event-goer to a believer in your cause. Sometimes this conversion happens at or after the event, so plan your event follow-up well if donor acquisition is one of your goals.

Your event could also focus on the mission and vision, with current community members bringing friends to the first point of contact and the beginning of a beautiful friendship? In this setting, you could feasibly foster donor retention while taking the first steps towards donor acquisition.

Your event goal will determine what type of event you hold, how you will gather sponsorship and attendees, and the engagement activities in the weeks and months that follow.

When you plan an event, be sure to plan your follow-up because, without appropriate follow-up, most events do not lead to a donor relationship and are merely an influx of cash without long term benefits.

- *Personal Ask*

Create an individualized personal solicitation plan for each high-end donor. Know how many prospects you have, who is the best person to ask them, and the time frame for the ask. Cultivation and stewardship are critical. Be realistic about how many personal asks you can make in a month, recognizing that not every call or in-person visit will result in an ask or a gift.

- *Small-Group Ask*

Enlist board members, major donors, volunteers, and staff to invite their friends and colleagues to an intimate gathering where you present the mission. Or create opportunities for specific segments of the donor base (major donors, monthly donors, donors to a particular program) to hear from an expert, discuss the topic, or brainstorm.

- *Peer-to-Peer Campaigns*

Find individuals closely tied to the organization—board members, staff, volunteers, and program participants to be ambassadors by reaching out to their family, friends, colleagues, and social media followers. Remember, not all donors act for the same reason. Some donors give because of their relationship with someone in your organization. Donating because of a personal connection to the person asking for support is the foundation of a peer-to-peer campaign.

Not every peer-to-peer fundraiser has the same network capacity, amount of time to dedicate to the campaign, or comfort level with reaching out. Allowing each participant to set their own right-sized goals for a given effort without fear of judgment for doing less than others increases enthusiasm. It offers participants a sense of ownership over the process.

- *Direct mail and e-mail*

As you create your fundraising plan, be sure to include _at least_ one direct mail piece (if you have postal address information) and three or four email campaigns (if you have email information). As we've already discussed, most organizations do not ask enough. Too many fear donor fatigue. I've heard of studies (I don't remember where) that say you can send more than twenty direct mail appeals and more than 80 emails before donors report fatigue. This seems excessive to me! But it gives us some indication that a few direct mail campaigns a year and at least one email campaign a quarter isn't too much!

You'll need to watch your donor engagement, and as I've mentioned, don't merely mail everyone on your list regardless of their previous engagement and response rate. Remember that if you can only communicate with a group through direct mail because you don't have other contact information, be sure to report impact a few times between appeals through newsletters or impact reports. Since email blasts don't usually cost per piece like direct mail, you can send them more often.

Ideally, you engage often enough with donors that each communication has one purpose or intention: to thank, to share positive impact, to inform on progress, or to ask for support.

If you are asking, don't spend the entire first paragraph thanking them for a previous gift or sharing how everyone and everything related to your organization is doing so wonderfully—leaving the ask for the last line of the letter. Even if you throw in catchy phrases like "because of your generosity," you risk losing their attention before they get to the section where you ask for support.

When you communicate via the written word, remember attention spans are short, but your communications don't need to be too brief. You have just a few seconds to grab a reader's attention, but a two-page direct mail appeal is often more effective than a shorter one. Emails should be more concise. Regardless of the format, you need to let the reader quickly know why they are receiving the letter or email.

And don't forget to use photos, large font, plenty of white space, bold, underline, and italics to guide the eye.

- *Social media*

Do you have a robust social media following? If so, using your social media platforms for fundraising can be very effective. When and how often will you do these? How much do you hope to raise from each one? Would Google Ads or a Facebook boost be appropriate? Should you join a crowdfunding platform (GoFundMe's charity.gofundme.com, mightycause.com, givey.com)? Would an online petition (ipetition.com, care2.com, yousignanimals.org) draw the attention of folks who care about your cause? Or are they likely to jump onto a gaming site (tiltify.com) to fundraise for you while they play a game?

I'm presenting questions here, do-gooder, because you'll need to decide how your community is likely to respond. If you aren't sure, try some of these ideas if you have the resources to do so.

* *Monthly Giving Program*

Whether you direct mail, email, call, meet in person, or reach someone through social media, don't be afraid to ask potential donors to become monthly donors to your cause. Encourage them to set-up recurring monthly contributions through your website, a giving platform like PayPal, or an automatic ACH bank transfer.

Monthly gifts are like magic. They're sustainable for the donor as they rarely have a significant impact on their monthly budget, but they've made a meaningful contribution over a year. And with a robust monthly giving program, your organization receives a monthly income that raises the valleys between the peaks provided through other fundraising campaigns. The combination of timely fundraising campaigns supported by ongoing monthly gifts creates sustainable support for your mission.

* *Phone or text-to-give*

Don't forget the device that almost everyone carries with them at all times. Trends show that more and more folks are likely to open and respond to a text message— especially the younger generations. So as you review your fundraising plans, consider what part text messaging will play in communicating with your donor base.

At the same time, don't forget the power of conversation. While many people don't answer their phones anymore, consider your community's age and attitudes when deciding whether to scrap making phone calls.

- *Planned or legacy giving program*

If you're a small or early-stage nonprofit, asking about estate planning may be premature, but as you grow and your organization gains credibility, don't be afraid to have a planned giving program in your fundraising portfolio.

Step 5. Calendar Your Itinerary

Once you clearly understand the channels you hope to use, you will need to review your Communications Plan to decide where you will be able to insert your various fundraising campaigns.

I would suggest beginning with the campaigns that will likely yield the highest return on investment. Hopefully, you'll be able to manage some type of fundraising campaign at least once a quarter. Ideally, you'd have something happening each month—with the personal solicitation visits with major donors an ongoing, consistent activity in your calendar.

- For each campaign, decide what channels you will use to achieve your goal.
- For each element of the campaign:
  o Determine the action steps to accomplish the objective.
  o How will you get it done?
  o How long will the objective take? Calendar the start date for each action step.
  o Who is responsible for making it happen?

Step 6. Transactional Honesty

Remember, you should not plan a campaign without scheduling the transactional follow-up that will lead to good stewardship. These steps take time and resources.

Revisit the gift acknowledgment policy you established in the 5th Commandment. What are the concrete steps for sending receipts, thanking, and stewarding the donors who attend and contribute to the various aspects of each campaign? Will your policy leave the attendees and donors feeling appreciated and likely to continue the relationship? Are those responsible for implementing the transactional steps to this policy informed and available to ensure it happens?

Step 7. Donor Stewardship

No fundraising plan is complete without a dedicated donor stewardship program. As we discussed in the 5th Commandment, when we talked about gratitude, your fundraising plan must be rooted in gratitude and expressing appreciation for those who contribute time, talent, and treasure to your organization.

Remember the critical elements of donor stewardship when you decide who, how, when, and how often to ask your supporters for donations.

P.S. To Sum It Up

Like a good P.S., I've pulled a list of one-liners to drive home the main points of the Ten Commandments that I hope will get you to your Promised Land.

- **Clarify your vision. Find your ONE mission.**
- Don't stray from WHY. Avoid mission creep.
- Make mission-centric decisions.
- Protect the organization from any one individual.
- **Confront structural racism and inequity.**
- Create a culture that respects boundaries & encourages well-being w/ grace & gratitude.
- Prepare for profitability. Manage your mission.
- Don't change for the heck of it. Don't remain stagnate.
- **Work smart, not hard.**
- Act quickly but not in a hurry.
- **Create a culture, not an attitude, of gratitude.**
- Don't be the invoice organization!
- **Communicate consistently. Ask authentically.**
- Don't brag like Narcissa.
- Be loyal. Don't be MIA.
- Stop begging. Don't treat donors like your ATM.
- Embrace transactional and relational honesty.
- Don't covet. Don't compare. Don't compete.
- **Keep calm and fundraise.**

Made in United States
Orlando, FL
31 January 2023

29320623R00148